GREAT CUSTOMER SERVICE
FOR YOUR
SMALL BUSINESS

by Richard F. Gerson, Ph

U.S. CHAMBER OF COMMERCE

SMALL
BUSINESS
INSTITUTE™

CREDITS

Editor: Beverly Manber

Layout/Design: ExecuStaff

Cover Design: Barry Littmann

Library of Congress 95-70898
ISBN-1-56052-364-6

**CRISP
PUBLICATIONS**

ABOUT THE USCC SMALL BUSINESS INSTITUTE

The U.S. Chamber of Commerce Small Business Institute was formed to provide practical education and training resources for small business professionals and employees. The Institute offers practical and informative materials in:

- Marketing and Sales

- Budgeting and Finance

- Legal Issues

- Human Relations and Communication

- Productivity

- Quality and Customer Service

- Supervision, Management and Leadership

These ready reference materials, created for the U.S. Chamber by Crisp Publications, contain a wealth of useful advice for small businesses. The personal involvement exercises provide an opportunity to immediately apply what has been learned to your business.

While learning, it is easy to earn a Small Business Institute Certificate of Completion and valuable Continuing Education Units (CEUs). For more information or to enroll, call 800-884-2880.

THE U.S. CHAMBER OF COMMERCE
SMALL BUSINESS INSTITUTE

► **High Quality**
Up-to-date and to-the-point training and educational materials are selected by small business professionals.

► **Practical and Easy to Use**
You can immediately put to use the proven tips and techniques.

► **Cost-effective**
The courses come to you—you don't have to spend money on travelling to a training site or pay costly tuition.

► **Design Your Own Program**
Choose those courses that interest you most and meet the specific needs of your company.

► **Self-paced**
Learn when your schedule permits. Complete the coursework on your time.

► **Recognition and Reward**
Business owners and employees can earn Continuing Education Units (CEUs) as well as a Small Business Institute Certificate of Completion to recognize the achievement.

► **Quality Guaranteed**
All materials are unconditionally guaranteed. If you are not totally satisfied, simply return course materials within 30 days for a complete refund. No questions asked.

DEDICATION

My family and my clients have taught me the importance of great service and its relationship to continued success. This book is dedicated with much love and gratitude to my wife, Robbie, my boys, Michael and Mitchell, and to all my clients. Thank you.

CONTENTS

CONTENTS (continued)

PREFACE

So much has been written about the importance of customer service. Today, no business can succeed for any length of time without offering great customer service. Years ago a business made a product and sold it to the customer. More often than not, it was a one-time transaction. If something went wrong, it was too bad for the customer.

Then, something happened. Customers became more educated and more demanding of the company and people they bought from. They wanted more value for their money. They wanted to reduce their purchase risks, so that if something went wrong with the purchase, they could return or exchange it. They refused to be pushed around any more by businesses. They wanted better customer service.

What did this mean for the small business owner? It opened a treasure chest of opportunities. While many large companies could not change their policies and procedures quickly enough to accommodate the customers, many small businesses immediately began giving customers what they wanted. Customer service began to level the playing field for small companies that sold the same items as their larger competitors.

Today, it seems that all competitors promote the superior quality and high levels of their customer service. Yet, not everyone can deliver on those promises. "Talking the talk" is no longer enough. Customers are too smart—we must "walk the talk that we talk," or customers will take their business somewhere else.

Every small business is capable of providing superior customer service and distinguishing itself from the competition. Management simply needs to recognize how important customer service is to the success of their business. In my book, *Marketing Strategies for Small Businesses*,[1] I suggest that any small business

---

[1] Crisp Publications, 1994.

can remain profitable, regardless of economic conditions, if they apply appropriate marketing strategies and tactics. Now, I am taking that bold statement a step further.

When you provide great customer service, you will survive no matter what happens to the economy or what competition moves into the neighborhood. People do business with people they like, and they usually like people who provide them courteous and friendly service. Customers are loyal to these people and their businesses, and continue to buy from them.

That is what this book is about. It shows small business owners in any industry how to implement user-friendly and results-oriented customer service systems. It describes how you can use customer service as a powerful marketing tool, and how you can measure the quality of your service along with your customers' levels of satisfaction. It teaches you how to develop the most important customer service skills you and your staff will need to dazzle and delight your customers. You'll learn the skills you need to use customer service as a marketing tool, to improve your listening and communication skills that are so important to service success, to handle the telephone properly, to manage complaints and turn them into sales, and to deal with angry customers. Finally, you'll learn a variety of techniques to retain customers for life.

Customer service is critical to the success of every small business. While great marketing will bring in customers for the first purchase, your level of service will keep them coming back. Every customer deserves a level of service that is ten times the amount of their purchase price. When you do this, you ensure their commitment and loyalty to your business; when you do not do this, your customers become someone else's customers.

Small business owners must establish and implement customer service systems and programs that are designed to help gain, and retain and keep customers for life. This book provides the blueprint.

Richard F. Gerson, Ph.D., CMC

CHAPTER ONE

GETTING AHEAD OF THE COMPETITION

JUMP START YOUR CUSTOMER SERVICE PROGRAMS

Being in business today is tough. Competitors are popping up from every angle. Each day you survive, it seems that someone else opens a business with the express purpose of taking away your customers.

Let me give you ten ways that you can jump-start your customer service programs and processes and put your business way ahead of your competition. Combine any or all of these ten customer service tips with some of the marketing tips at the beginning of my book, *Marketing Strategies for Small Businesses*,[2] and you will supercharge your business. In fact, you will notice that a few of the customer service and marketing techniques overlap. This is by design: when you put great service together with great marketing, you end up with an unbeatable combination.

TEN GREAT CUSTOMER SERVICE AND CUSTOMER RETENTION TIPS

1. Unique Service Philosophy

If you have read *Marketing Strategies for Small Businesses*[3], you know how important a Unique Selling Proposition (USP) is to the success of your business. The USP tells customers why you are different and better than your competitors. It is what makes you stand out from the crowd, and is the main reason customers should do business with you.

The Unique Service Philosophy is another statement of how you do business. It tells customers what they can expect to receive from you in the way of great customer service. It also tells your employees, and your competitors, how customers will be treated when they do business with you.

---

[2]Crisp Publications, 1994.
[3]Crisp Publications, 1994.

Developing your Unique Service Philosophy is not as easy as it may sound or seem. You can begin by writing down your random thoughts on the topic. Do not be concerned about grammar, language, sentence structure or anything else. Your first goal is to put your thoughts on paper so you can look at them and then organize them.

Once you write down your initial thoughts, arrange them so they make sense. Remember that your service philosophy must describe how you will take care of your customers and what your customers will receive from you. Part of your philosophy should answer the "WIIFM" question for your customers: "What's In It For Me?"

Your Turn

Answer the following question:

► What can your customers expect to receive from you in the way of great customer service?

My company's service philosophy is comprehensive and quite lengthy. It will give you an idea of the level of commitment we have to quality customer service. Feel free to adapt the ideas in our philosophy to your business and company.

Our Unique Service Philosophy is on page 5. When you develop yours, make certain you communicate it in everything you do: your words, your letters and your actions. Many businesses' products, pricing, guarantees and warranties are similar to their competitor's. The thing that differentiates one company from the next is its approach to customer service. Communicating your Unique Service Philosophy to customers will help them decide to do business with you instead of your competitors. After all, *wouldn't you want to do business with someone who will give you great service and do whatever it takes to satisfy you?*

Service Philosophy of Gerson Goodson, Inc.

It is our customer service philosophy to be available, adaptable, flexible and responsive to the needs, wants and expectations of our customers and clients. We achieve this by listening carefully to what our customers tell us, by asking (even begging) for feedback from our customers, making changes in our policies, procedures and performances based on customer recommendations and suggestions, and then giving customers exactly what they want and ask for, and something extra.

Our goal is to always exceed our customers' expectations of us. At a minimum, we do whatever it takes to meet customer expectations and satisfy the customer. At a maximum, we do whatever we can to delight and dazzle our customers.

We realize, of course, that no company or person is perfect. There will be times when whatever we are able to do still does not delight and dazzle the customer. At those times, we ask the customer to tell us exactly what we must do to satisfy them. After we listen, we do it.

If for some reason the customer is still not satisfied, and we have done everything within our power, we work with the customer to find someone who can satisfy those needs and wants and expectations that we were unable to meet. The goal here is not to find fault or to blame either Gerson Goodson, Inc., or the customer. The goal is to do whatever it takes to satisfy the customer.

That is our customer service philosophy. Do whatever it takes to satisfy all customers and clients. Do it right the first time. Do it as often as the customer requires it. And, if we can't deliver for some reason, find a colleague or even a competitor who can meet and exceed our customer's expectations.

It is this approach to customer service that has made Gerson Goodson, Inc. so successful, and we will continue to adhere to this philosophy. We also work with our customers to create a win-win partnership to help them develop a similar philosophy and approach to customer service so everyone achieves long-lasting success.

Your Turn

Write your Unique Service Philosophy for your business.

If you are still having trouble coming up with your Unique Service Philosophy, here is a little help. Your company should have a mission statement, which is simply the reason and purpose you're in business. If your company does not have a mission statement, start writing one now.

Your Turn

Write your mission statement for your business.

Assuming you have a mission statement, take a close look at that statement and identify all the parts of it that talk about you, your company and your employees.

Your Turn

Answer the following questions:

► Is there anything in your company's mission statement that talks about the customer? (There should be.)

► List all the important values you have in your business and your personal life. These values can include honesty, integrity, service, communication, friendship, positive relationships, etc.

► Where on your list of values do you have service and helping others?

► Combine the service values with the service aspects of your mission statement. Don't worry about the grammar or the sentence structure. Just get the ideas down on paper.

▶ Read through what you wrote again.

▶ Does it start to form a picture of what makes your business unique in the way of service? When it does, write out your Unique Service Philosophy. Again, feel free to adapt my company's statement to suit your needs.

My company does not have a mission statement. We have a *Customer Commitment* statement, which helps us stay in touch with our customers and keeps our Unique Service Philosophy focused. In actuality, it is a mission statement combined with some values statements. We call it our Customer Commitment statement so we never forget who is important to our success in business.

2. Customer Feedback

Customer feedback is critical to your success in providing great customer service. How do you know what customers think of you, your business, the product or service you sold them, and anything else related to your business? You don't unless you take the steps to find out.

Ask customers for their feedback. Beg them for it, if you have to. Do whatever you must to get them to tell you how they see you, think about you, and feel about you. Set up customer councils, advisory boards, mail out questionnaires, do telephone surveys, ask customers to fill out postcards when they make a purchase, and interview them personally.

When you get this information from them, identify where you can improve. The gaps in service performance are the keys to your future success. Here are some of the service gaps that you will probably encounter, and that you need to close:

▶ Not knowing what customers need and want from you and what they expect of you

▶ A difference between what customers believe they received from you and what you believe you delivered

- A difference between the way you think customers want to be treated and the way they actually want to be treated

- A difference between your expectations of service quality performance and the customer's expectations

- A difference between what you promise to deliver and what you actually deliver

You can probably think of several more gaps that need to be closed. If you cannot, your customers will identify them for you. The key is to close these gaps as quickly as possible. The faster you address these issues, the more satisfied your customers will be. Plus, when they see that you take care of the service issues they raised, they will be more motivated to continue doing business with you regularly. Only when a business does not address issues brought up by customers does the business begin to lose those customers to competitors.

Here is a hint. Shop your competitors and find out exactly what they are doing to solicit customer feedback and close their gaps. Then, do the same thing, plus one thing more. When customers learn that they get more service from you for the same dollar they spend, they will bring more business to you.

3. Customer Retention Programs

Do whatever it takes to keep the customer. Later, you will learn several methods you can use to keep customers for life. Your goal is to "close the back door," because it costs five or six times as much to get a new customer as it does to do business with a customer you keep.

Here are few ways to retain your customers:

- Get them involved with your business. Customer councils and advisory boards are excellent tools.

- Have a Customer Appreciation Day or week.

- Run special sales or offer special services.

- ► Ask customers how you can serve them better and then give them what they tell you.

- ► Keep your name in front of customers by using newsletters, letters of news, key chains, magnets, calendars, and anything else you can think of.

I know one business that, at the beginning of the year, sends its customers a small gift bag of homemade, 4-ounce chocolate chip cookies with a note that says to have a sweet and successful year. Even if you do not like the cookies, you have to appreciate the thought and the effort.

I have trained hundreds of clients to make "Hello, how are you?" calls to retain their customers. These calls have no sales attached to them. They are simply telephone calls to find out how the customers are doing. The calls can be short and to the point. The customers know that you took the time to think of them.

These little extra efforts on your part go a long way to retain customers. If your customers stay with you, they cannot go to your competitors. Your competitors' customers will likely hear about what you do and may even become your customers. Getting involved in customer retention programs as part of your overall customer service system can pay double dividends.

4. Know Your Customers Intimately

Many businesses claim to know their customers, but, how many businesses know their customers *intimately*?

I use a contact management computer software program to keep track of all the information I will ever need on each of my customers. For example, I know when we first meet or speak, exactly what we talk about, what each of us is supposed to do following each meeting or conversation, the school they graduated from, the names of their spouses and children, who their secretary is, whom they report to, who else makes decisions with them, and many other pieces of information. I find all this out by asking customers specific questions, carefully listening to their answers, and taking notes during our conversations.

Imagine a customer coming in to see you or calling you on the phone and asking you about something that occurred between the two of you nine months ago. You check your computer and you know exactly what he or she is talking about. Or, if you know in advance they will be coming in, you can pull up all the information you need to have for the meeting. You look like a genius.

You can also get to know your prospects intimately, and this helps transform them into customers. I met someone who represented a great deal of business for my company. I knew they like football (it came up several times during our conversations) and that they could not get tickets to a game. A friend of mine who had season tickets offered me two for a specific game he could not make. I paid him for the tickets and sent them to my prospect with a note saying that he should use them and enjoy himself. The end-result was that this prospect became a satisfied customer.

I knew of his love for football because I asked the proper questions and listened carefully for the answers. Do this with both prospects and customers. Know them intimately. They will appreciate your desire to learn more about them and will reward you with more business.

5. Meet and Exceed Expectations

This concept will come up over and over again throughout the book. Find out exactly what customers expect of you, and do what it takes to meet and exceed those expectations. By meeting expectations, you create a satisfied customer. When you exceed expectations, you create a dazzled and delighted customer who refers business to you.

Your competitors are promoting the fact that they provide great customer service and meet their customers' expectations. To stand out and apart from your competitors, you must exceed your customers' expectations every chance you get. One way to do this is to ask your customers what they expect of you. Ask them personally, on the phone, by mail, or any way you can think of. Then go out and exceed their expectations. They will love you for your efforts.

6. Customer Reward and Recognition Programs

What gets rewarded gets done. Everyone in the world wants to be shown appreciation. Children thrive on it, and adults do also. As adults, we usually put this need on a back burner. The truth is, though, that adults do need to be appreciated and will accomplish remarkable things if they know their efforts are being recognized and appreciated. Recognize customers for their positive (e.g., purchasing/buying/referring) behaviors and they will continue to do business with you.

Set up your recognition and reward programs to benefit your customers. Make certain what you provide for them is perceived as valuable and genuinely given. When you make a person feel special, they will do what they can to return to the source of that special feeling. In this case, it means doing business with you again.

Create a program for your employees similar to the recognition and reward program you set up for your customers. They are the source of your great customer service, and they will do the best job when you reward their efforts.

Rewards do not have to be financial. Psychological rewards often have a more powerful and long-lasting effect. Money and present eventually disappear. Emotional rewards last forever.

This example of the greatest recognition/reward I have ever received is personal and not business-oriented. However, you can adapt the concept to your business.

> My wife gave me an unbelievable present for my fortieth birthday. Most people get jewelry, cars, and other material things for their birthdays. My wife rented a hotel suite on the Gulf of Mexico, had a private chef make dinner for us, and arranged for someone to watch the children for the evening. We had the most beautiful and enjoyable evening anyone could imagine.

When I asked her why she gave this to me as a birthday present instead of the more typical gifts, she said that those gifts would eventually become passé. This gift would last a lifetime. And, she is right. The memory is still positive, powerful and will be with me forever.

Your Turn

Answer the following question:

▶ How can you adapt this idea to your business?

---

7. Continuously Improve the Service Process

Remember that the process you use to provide great customer service can always be improved. You have probably heard the saying, "If it ain't broke, don't fix it." I am here to tell you that if it ain't broke, you better break it and make it better.

Have you ever broken a bone in your finger or foot? You may have read about an athlete who returned to his or her sport in better shape than before, after rehabilitation for an injury. Usually, when an injury heals, the body is stronger than before.

The same holds true for your business. You may be cruising along providing great customer service and making a nice profit. You tend to get comfortable in what you are doing. The next thing you know, your competition has come up with some type of value-added service and your customers are flocking to that business. That is why you must continually improve your service processes. Do not rest on your laurels or on previous comments from customers. Continue to get their feedback and find ways to do what you do even better.

One way you can begin to continuously improve your service process is to begin measuring everything you do. You can measure things like:

- ▶ Answering the telephone by the fourth ring

- ▶ Keeping a caller on hold for no more than 30 seconds before getting back to him or her

- ▶ Returning telephone calls within 24 hours

- ▶ Responding to written correspondence within 24 hours

- ▶ Sending a technician to a site within 3 hours

- ▶ Shipping orders within 24 hours

- ▶ Sending replacement parts within 12 hours

- ▶ Same-day service.

You get the idea.

Remember that if you do not or cannot measure it, you cannot improve it. If you are having difficulty developing measurements for your service performances (and this happens often because services are intangible), ask your employees for help. Not only will they come up with objective measurement standards, they will be more likely to accept and buy-in to those standards since they had a role in developing them. Chart these measurements for everyone to see. Over time, natural human behavior will lead to improvements, because you have made the measurements visible.

You can also use these measurements to create improvement programs. This is the basis of the total quality management approach to business. What gets measured gets done; and what gets measured gets improved. This is especially true about service performance. Use this simple chart to help you start to develop your service standards of performance.

GOAL	BEHAVIOR	STANDARD

Many people believe—incorrectly—that service performance cannot be measured because it deals with an intangible and with perceptions. There are aspects of service performance you can measure. The key is to develop objective standards you can use to measure various types of service performance.

Your key to success for continuously improving your service processes is accurate and ongoing measurements. You now have several ways to measure your service quality and customer satisfaction. Put them to use immediately! For more information on how to make these measurements and apply them to the continuous improvement process, see my book *Measuring Customer Satisfaction.*[4]

---

[4]Crisp Publications, 1993.

8. Service Psychology

This concept is both a service technique and a mindset. If you and your people do not have a service mentality, then everything you try to do with regard to customer service will be hindered. Everyone must realize that everyone involved in the business is a customer service representative. Service is not someone else's job. It is your job, and it is everyone's job. Once this mindset is established, you can provide superior customer service. An extension of this mindset is how you perceive your business in comparison to how customers perceive it.

Your Turn

Answer the following questions:

► What image and identity do you hold for your business?

► Is this the same image and identity that customers have of it?

For a customer to feel good about doing business with you, that customer must believe that your product or service improves or enhances his or her personal image, self esteem or ego. At the very least, buying from you must help the customer maintain the status quo. No customer wants to buy a product or service from someone if the purchase makes that customer feel less important or if the person who sold them the product "brings them down" in some way.

The image and identity you create in your community influences when, how often and how long customers buy from you. You can volunteer and support charities or sponsor youth sports teams as a way to boost your community image and increase your community service. When customers see you doing these things, they enjoy doing business with you because it makes them feel good. They feel good about your support for the community and they feel good about themselves for doing business with someone who is so supportive. Some people even feel that they are vicariously supporting the community or the charity when they buy from you.

These examples illustrate the importance of a positive psychological mindset towards customer service. When everyone in your business has this mindset, they will naturally provide great service to your customers.

9. Make Service Systems Easily Accessible and User Friendly

Your Turn

Answer the following questions:

► Have you ever heard someone say they could do a great job if it were not for the customers?

► Have you or your employees ever said it?

That is a frightening thought, especially when you consider that your customers are the only reason you are in business. Time and again I have seen businesses in which customer service systems are set up to make it easier for employees to do their jobs. Policies and procedures, rules and regulations guide the employees in how to deal with customers. If a situation comes up that is not in the "book," the employee says nothing can be done because it is not in the book or is not the way they do things.

Can you imagine that? Today with customers switching loyalties at the drop of a hat, some businesses still do what they can to alienate customers. Make all your customer service systems easy for the customer to use. Your employees must realize that their primary job is to satisfy and keep the customers. This means that they must be prepared to handle complaints and resolve them to the customers' satisfaction. Train employees not to view complaints as something negative, but as opportunities to do something positive for the customers and to cement customers' loyalty. The more loyal customers you have, the more profitable your business will be; it costs far less to market to customers and to get them to buy from you again than it does to develop a new customer.

10. Train and Empower Your Employees

If your company has too many rules and regulations about how to deal with customers—notice I did not say serve or satisfy—destroy your rule book. Employees cannot do the best job possible for you if they work handcuffed. That is what all the rules do to them—rules can prevent them from doing their job well.

I am not saying your business should not have rules or policies to guide it and the employees in how to conduct the business. I am saying you should review what you already have in place and see what you can cut out. Remove any rules and regulations, policies and procedures that prevent or even hold back your employees from doing a great job for your customers.

Your Turn

Answer the following question:

► Does your business have rules, regulations, policies or procedures that prevent employees from doing a great job for your customers?

This is the essence of empowerment. Provide employees with the authority and responsibility to do whatever it takes to satisfy your customers. Train your employees to do this well. This moves them from empowerment to enablement. If rules have to be "broken or bent" for a specific situation, your employees should know they have the leeway to bend the rules. If a situation is not covered in one of the books, train them well enough so they can make decisions on their own. Then, support their decisions.

Making a decision that is supported by the owner or top management does more to motivate an employee to continue to perform well than any other incentive program. In a television commercial for Saturn cars, an assembly line worker expresses his surprise at receiving the authority (empowerment) to stop the line if he finds something wrong with a car. He has never stopped the line before, so he is unsure of the "repercussions" if he pulls the rope. When he stops the line and his supervisor supports his decision, he stands tall and tells how proud he is to work at Saturn.

Your Turn

Answer the following question:

► How can you adapt this atmosphere, feeling and concept to your business?

Train your employees to do their jobs well and right, and to serve and satisfy the customers to the best of their abilities. Give them the authority and responsibility to do whatever it takes to make a customer happy. Support their decisions in these matters, especially in front of customers.

You may be worried that your employees may give away the store if you empower them. If so, you are worrying needlessly. Most, if not all employees, look out for the general welfare and well-being of the business. They will not give away the store and they will not "bite the hand that feeds them."

These are ten ideas to provide superior customer service and retain your customers. Begin implementing several of these ideas simultaneously. You may never get all ten implemented or running at one time. That is fine. Just try to get as many going as you can. You will begin to see more satisfied customers frequent your business more often and buy more from you. Plus, they will refer more new people to you.

ASK YOURSELF

► What will you do to improve your Unique Service Philosophy?

► Describe the service gaps in your business.

► Identify at least five steps you will take to get to know your customers more intimately.

WHAT
CUSTOMERS
REALLY
NEED,
WANT AND
EXPECT

QUALITY SERVICE AND SATIS-FACTION

The definitions *quality service* and *customer satisfaction* are the same: *whatever the customer says they are.*

Superior customer service requires you to be effective—to do the right things right at the right time. Superior customer service is not doing things right—that is efficiency. If this sounds like it is just a matter of semantics, think again. It is not semantics in your customers' minds. They want you to do what is right for them and by them, as they define it.

You must know exactly what customers need from you, what they want as a result of doing business with you, and what they expect throughout the business transaction and your ongoing relationship with them.

The only way you will know what they think and want is to ask them. Many businesses think they know exactly what customers want from them. When they "give it" to their customers, they discover they guessed wrong. They end up either in trouble or out of business altogether.

You do not have to make any assumptions in business. Just ask your customers whatever you want to know, they will be happy to tell you. If you do not have any customers yet, because you are starting out, ask the customers of competitors what they want in the way of great customer service. They will be only too happy to tell you. You will probably also uncover some unmet needs on the part of your competitor's customers. When you can satisfy those needs, you can win the customers over to your business.

Here are ten needs that all customers have in one capacity or another. Do not consider this list complete or perfect for your business. Modify it, add and delete items, and adapt it to make it work for your business. This list is just a starting point.

Customers need from you:

► Help

► Respect

- ▶ Comfort

- ▶ Empathy and to be Heard

- ▶ Satisfaction

- ▶ Support

- ▶ A Friendly Face

- ▶ Understanding

- ▶ To Feel Important

- ▶ A Quality Product or Service at a Fair Price

These are some of the things customers *need* from you. What they *want* may be totally different. Do not confuse the two items. Needs are "got to have" things. Wants are "nice to have" things. For example, if you have holes in the bottom of your shoes, you need a pair of shoes. You may want a $200 pair of Italian soft leather shoes, but that is not what you need. You need a pair of shoes.

The difference is that needs can almost be made tangible, while wants are more psychological. If this sounds like we are getting too far afield, don't worry. All you need to do is ask your customers what they need and want from you. They will tell you, and if they confuse needs and wants, ask them to clarify.

You also must be clear on customers' expectations of you. Expectations refer to how well you meet the customers' criteria for successful performance. Expectations have nothing to do with you or what you are doing from your perspective; they are solely the customer's perspective.

If a customer expects you to call within two hours, and you call the next day, you have clearly not met his or her expectations. Think about how you feel when you wait for a table in a restaurant. If you are told the wait will only be ten minutes and you are still waiting twenty minutes later, your expectations of wait time have not been met. You begin to have a variety of negative thoughts about the restaurant. Even when you are seated, you begin your meal with a negative attitude that may affect your entire dining experience.

To determine your customers' expectations of you and for doing business with you, ask them directly. Use interviews, focus groups, telephone or written surveys, or other types of questionnaires. Do something to get them to communicate their expectations to you. You will learn more about alternative techniques to determine customer expectations later in this book.

DETERMINING HOW TO SATISFY CUSTOMERS

Questioning customers will give you some insight into what they need, want and expect of you. You also need to do some introspection regarding your own business. Ask yourself these questions about your customers and your business to determine how you think they perceive doing business with you:

▶ What result or benefit will customers receive from owning my product or buying my service?

▶ What is a customer's need level for my product or service?

▶ How important is my product or service to the customer? (What need or want does it satisfy?)

▶ What are the perceived costs and perceived risks the customer has related to owning my product or using my service?

▶ What does the customer want me to do to maintain his or her loyalty to my business?

 *Your Turn*   ***Answer the following question:***

▶ How can you modify these questions so that you can ask them of your customers?

Once you answer these questions, you will have a pretty good idea of how to satisfy your customers. Of course, your best knowledge will come from asking them what they expect of you. Remember, the only way to know exactly what you must do to satisfy your customers is to ask them directly.

In the past, if you provided good customer service, customers would seek you out instead of your competitors. Then, everyone started improving their service. Now, service cannot be used as a differentiating factor. So, companies have come up with other ways to enhance both the products and services they provide and the customer service that goes along with them. They call this value-added service.

The problem is that competitors have caught up quickly. When a company is capable of meeting a customer's expectations of service, that is now only the ante into the game. Good—even great—customer service only lets you stay in the game and levels the playing field. To be successful, you must provide "greater than great" customer service. You must consistently exceed their expectations so they come away from doing business with you saying, "Wow!" Quite simply, you must dazzle and delight your customers every chance you have.

Look at the Customer Expectations Model below. It looks like a basic organizational chart, except that the blank spaces are for areas of your business, rather than people and positions.

Customer Expectations Model

Customer Expectations

Your Turn

► Fill in the blanks with areas of your business that customers will hold expectations of you for performance. (You may not have five areas at this time.) For example, you might write Administration in one box, Marketing in another, Sales in a third, and Operations in a fourth.

► Identify areas under each category heading that act as sub-headings. These sub-headings are the actual behaviors that customers will expect from you. For example, for the Sales category, your sub-headings might include courtesy of the sales person, on-time delivery of the product or service, after sale service, and one contact person for problem resolution or future sales.

When you complete the Customer Expectations Model for each category, you go way beyond what your competitors are doing. You are able to more accurately determine exactly what your customers expect of you, and you can tailor your performance and those of your employees to meet and exceed those expectations. You also have five areas of opportunity in which to create the Wow Factor.

How to Get the Wow Factor

Customers will say "Wow!" based on what you do for them that they never expected. However, you must start this process well before you interact with customers. You need to improve your awareness of certain things related to customers and customer service, and develop an understanding of specific behaviors customers often evidence.

Let's begin your Wow Factor training with developing and increasing your awareness.

Superior service providers are aware of many things, some too numerous to mention. The following list of ideas will give you a head start over your competition. The list applies to you, to your employees and to your customers.

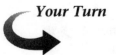

Your Turn

► After each item on the list, fill in some information that clarifies the item. Customize the list to your specific business.

► Share your list with your staff as a profit-producing, internal marketing activity.

Be aware of the following:

1. Attitudes

2. Behaviors

3. Concerns

4. Desires, Wants and Wishes

5. Expectations and Intentions

6. Perceptions

7. Physical State

8. Mental State

9. Physical State Affecting Mental State and Vice Versa

10. Influencers, such as Family and Friends

11. Your Personal Appearance

12. Business Appearance and Environment

13. Communication

14. Availability and Accessibility of Staff

15. Costs

16. _____

17. _____

18. _____

19. _____

20. _____

TEN TYPES OF CUSTOMER BEHAVIORS

Once you increase your awareness toward how to create the Wow Factor, you need to understand how customers behave when they do business with you. For each of the following ten behavior patterns you will encounter from customers, consider what you must do to work with and satisfy each type of customer.

1. *The Superior, Know-It-All Customer*

   This person knows your business better than you do and will not hesitate to tell you and anyone else who will listen.

2. *The Resistive Customer*

   No matter what you try to do for this person, he or she will resist every effort on your part to satisfy them. It is almost as if they love making themselves and others miserable, or at least stressing people out.

3. *The Dependent Customer*

   This customer is like a newborn infant who is totally dependent on a parent. These types of customers want you to do everything for them and will not lift a finger to help themselves.

4. *The Hostile/Antagonistic Customer*

   Here is the customer who loves to pick a fight or an argument, or simply wants to stir things up. He or she is not having a bad day, but a bad life and taking it out on everyone they meet. Be careful as this customer can become verbally and physically abusive.

5. *The Depressed Customer*

   Even though nothing you do seems to satisfy this customer, have pity for anyone who is always sad. While you may spend some time listening to this customer's problems, do not become their therapist.

6. *The Quiet and Uncommunicative Customer*

It is hard to know how to satisfy someone when they do not tell you what you need to know.

7. *The Talkative Customer*

Although they probably just want someone to listen to them, their constant babbling can really become annoying. While you have to come up with a way to quiet them down, do it without insulting them or shattering their self-esteem.

8. *The Let-Others-Speak-For-Me Customer*

Here is a person who will not say a word to you, but has friends and family act as the go-between.

9. *The Chronic Complainer*

We all know about this customer. While this customer is probably a combination of several of the other types, he and she deserve a separate mention. They buy, they complain and they return what they bought. Or they want a refund. Or, they want to chew your head off. Whatever you do, they are never going to be happy.

10. *The Perfect Customer*

Here is the person who buys from you and is so satisfied with the purchase, they recommend you and refer you to other customers. When this customer complains, it is to provide you with feedback so you can improve your service to them the next time. Find your perfect customers; ask them what they love about doing business with you; and then ask them for referrals.

There you have it. Ten types of customer behaviors to be on the look-out for. Determine how you and your staff will handle each type. It is important for you to know what to do, because you will encounter these people several times each day. Since customers are the lifeblood of your business, you cannot run away from them. Learn who these people are and find out how to meet and exceed their expectations. Do whatever it takes, within reason, to dazzle and delight them. When they conduct business with you, have them leave the situation saying, "Wow!"

ASK YOURSELF

► Define customer satisfaction in your business.

► Describe what you plan to do to satisfy the expectations that customers have of you and your business.

► Explain what you will do to get the Wow factor into your business.

► Identify the type of customers you encounter most often. How have you handled them in the past, and what changes will you make in how you handle them?

THE
IMPORTANCE
OF
CUSTOMER
SERVICE

CHAPTER THREE

CUSTOMER SERVICE IS CRITICAL

Customer service is the critical factor for succeeding in business today. You must provide customer service that is far superior to that offered by your competitors, so your small business will attract and keep customers who remain loyal and help you make a profit.

A great deal has been written and said about customer service and how businesses should treat their customers. Despite all the books, articles, audio tapes and videos on the topic, thousands of businesses still have not gotten the message. And it is an easy message to get.

Much of customer service comes down to plain old common sense. Simply put, customer service involves everything you and your employees do to satisfy customers. That means you give them what they want and make sure they are happy when they leave. If you just manage complaints, offer refunds or exchanges on returns, and smile at customers, you only provide a small part of excellent customer service. Customer service also means going out of your way for the customer, doing everything possible to satisfy the customer, and making decisions that benefit the customer—sometimes even at the expense of the business. (If this happens, be sure you consider the future potential of that customer's business with you.)

Now, do not believe for a minute that I am saying you should give away the store to the customer. I am saying you must know when and how often the customer is right. You have probably heard that the customer is always right. Well, this is not actually the truth. Sometimes the customer is wrong, such as when they try to take advantage of you or become disruptive or abusive. Then, they definitely are not right. While they may not always be right, *they are always the customer.*

With this concept in mind, make all your service decisions based on the situation, what the customer wants, and how it affects your business. Treat every customer the way he or she wants to be treated. Interact with each customer as an individual. Treat every service situation as unique. Do not let inflexible rules and regulations, policies and procedures stop you from making your customers happy.

THE IMPORTANCE OF CUSTOMER SERVICE

How important is customer service to the success of your business? It can literally make or break you. Consider this. You and your competitors are selling the same product or service at basically the same price. Nothing within the product or service really differentiates you from each other. This being the case, what makes customers buy from you instead of your competitors?

Could it be the way you and your employees treat them? How about the way you answer the telephone, or listen to their requests for information on what you are selling? What about the appearance of your store or office? What about the service you provide after the sale? All these things relate to customer service and the impressions customers have of you. If these impressions and perceptions are positive, they probably will do business with you. If they are negative, or if you have done something to upset a customer, you can be sure he or she will go down the street to one of your competitors.

Think about the last time you had poor service. Perhaps it happened at a restaurant, an airport, a retail store or a health club. Remember what you thought and how you felt. Why would you want your customers to experience any of those negative or painful feelings? You know how you perceived the situation and what you planned to do about it. If you decided to take your business elsewhere, do you think your customers will do the same? Most customers will not complain. They will just "vote with their feet."

Using common sense to provide superior customer service simply means you and your staff will be nice to your customers. Treat them as you want to be treated. Better still, treat them as they want to be treated. Then, give them something extra to surprise them—something they did not expect. They will love you for it.

The Payoff of Superior Customer Service

Several years ago, you could not pay some small businesses to train their employees to provide good customer service. Either the businesses did not view customer service as important, or they did not think the training was important, or they did not think the employees warranted training beyond specific job skills. Some businesses I have worked with in the past actually felt that customers would come in, buy and leave, and it really did not matter if you were nice to them or not.

While there was a time when people would just accept how you treated them and continue to do business with you, that is no longer true. People are more educated, more value conscious, and they demand more for their dollar. If you do not provide them with great customer service, they will find someone who will.

Customer service pays. Yes, you may have to spend some dollars in training programs for your staff. And you may have some other expenses for revamping or revising your service delivery systems. But, in the long run, customer service always pays off. The way it pays off the most is in long-term customer retention. Keeping customers and doing business with them repeatedly is much less expensive and much more profitable than trying to find new customers all the time.

The Dollar Value of Customer Service

Some small businesses know the cost of acquiring a new customer, while others do not have a clue what new customer acquisition costs them. Furthermore, many business owners are not even aware of the extraordinary costs of losing a customer. They just figure that if someone stops doing business with them one day, another person will begin. Wrong! Later in this chapter, you will learn how to calculate both customer acquisition costs and the cost of poor service. Small businesses that know what it costs to acquire a customer are bending over backwards to keep them happy.

Here are three things you must know about the payoff for providing excellent customer service. First, it costs five to six times more to acquire a new customer than it does to do business with a current or former customer. So, if you were able to calculate the cost of acquiring a new customer, and let's say that it is $500, and you figure out that it only costs you about $100 to do business with an old customer, that is a $400 savings that becomes profit in your business.

Second, whenever you lose a customer, there are costs associated with replacing them, plus the loss of revenue their business would have provided during the replacement period, and something we call lost opportunity revenue. This is all the potential money you could have made from the customer if you kept them loyal and they continued to purchase from you over an extended period of time. These calculations will be provided on page 45.

The third thing is the cost of negative word-of-mouth. When you lose a customer, it is usually due to a bad experience they had with you. You can control between 96 and 99 percent of the reasons people stop doing business with you, depending on your type of business. So, in reality, you should only lose a small number of customers. But, if you dissatisfy even one customer, that person may tell up to twenty people about the bad service they received. The odds are these twenty people will not do business with you at all. Calculate that lost opportunity revenue over a three-, five- or ten-year period.

Add the costs of these three reasons together and you get a pretty good idea of how valuable and profitable it is to provide superior customer service, or how very costly it would be if you provided poor service. With this in mind, the question you should ask yourself is not whether you can afford to train your staff to provide excellent customer service, but can you really afford not to? Compare the payoff in money earned or saved by keeping your customers against what it costs you when you lose them.

To put it very simply, customer service and long-term customer retention and satisfaction are vitally important to your success in business.

Common Sense Customer Service

High quality customer service is as much a marketing tool for your business as it is a management approach or philosophy. Service quality improves your marketing because it motivates customers to tell others about you. These referrals essentially create a customer sales force. Remember, the least expensive way to acquire new customers is through word-of-mouth referrals. What better way to get new customers than have their friends tell them to do business with you. We will talk more about this concept later. For now, let's agree that it is just good common sense to provide superior customer service.

Good service also improves and makes management easier, because everybody is committed to satisfying the customer. Employees are happier knowing they can do whatever it takes to satisfy the customer without fear of reprisal or repercussions. This obviously makes customers happier. The results are increased satisfaction and referrals on the part of customers; increased productivity from employees; and increased profitability for the business, simply because everyone is working toward the same goal: customer satisfaction and retention.

Now that you know how important great customer service is to your success in business, let's get to the heart of the matter: money. The remainder of this chapter provides you with what I call *Startling Service Statistics*, gathered from a variety of research sources; a formula for calculating the costs of poor service and relating that to customer acquisition; and information on a little-known service/marketing concept combination called Lifetime Value of a Customer plus marginal net worth.

If this information does not motivate you to provide the ultimate in customer service, think about what you will do when your competitors steal your customers from you.

STARTLING SERVICE STATISTICS

Customers today are better educated than ever before. They are more careful about their purchases and the dollars they spend. They want value for their money. They also want good service and they are willing to pay for it. But who are these customers, and how do you know when they are happy?

► Only 4 percent of customers ever complain. That means your business may never hear from 96 percent of your customers, and 91 percent of those just go away because they feel complaining will not do them any good. Complainers are more likely to continue doing business with you than noncomplainers.

► For every complaint your business receives, there are twenty-six other customers with unresolved complaints or problems, and six of those customers have serious problems. These are people you probably will never hear from. These are also people who can tell you how to make your business better. Get their feedback any way you can.

► Most customers who complain to you (54 to 70 percent) will do business with you again if you resolve their complaint. If they feel you acted quickly and to their satisfaction, up to 95 percent of them will do business with you again, and they probably will refer other people to you.

► A dissatisfied customer will tell up to 10 people about it. Approximately 13 percent of those will tell up to 20 people about their problem. You cannot afford the advertising required to overcome this negative word-of-mouth.

► Happy customers or customers who have had their complaints resolved will tell between 3 and 5 people about their positive experiences. Therefore, you have to satisfy 3 to 4 customers for every customer who is dissatisfied with you.

It is difficult in any business to work with a 4:1 ratio against you. Customer retention programs enhance the value of your customer service efforts.

▶ It costs five to six times more to attract new customers than to keep old ones. Yet, when you go back and renew contacts with former customers and get them to do business with you again, these costs drop dramatically. Additionally, customer loyalty and the lifetime value of a customer can be worth up to ten times as much as the price of a single purchase.

▶ Businesses that provide superior customer service can charge more, realize greater profits, increase their market share, and have customers willingly pay more for their products, simply because of the good service. In fact, you can gain an average of six percent a year in market share, simply by providing good service that satisfies and keeps your customers.

▶ The lifetime value of a customer or the amount of purchases that customer would make over a 10-year period is worth more than the cost of returning the purchase price of one item.

For example, supermarkets realize up to $5,000 a year from one family. That means $50,000 over 10 years. Is it worth it for a supermarket to provide refunds when the customer returns a purchase? Is it worth it to you to have the good will and positive word-of-mouth this type of retention service will bring you?

▶ Customer service is governed by the rule of 10s: If it costs $10,000 to get a new customer, it takes only 10 seconds to lose one, and 10 years to get over it or for the problem to be resolved. You must work to keep your customers.

▶ Customers stop doing business with you because:

- 1% die

- 3% move away

- 5% seek alternatives or develop other business relationships

- 9% begin doing business with the competition

- 14% are dissatisfied with the product or service

- 68% are upset with the treatment they have received

If you look at these percentages, you actually have some control over 96–99 percent of the reasons customers stop doing business with you.

The Cost of Poor Service

Have you figured out what poor customer service is actually costing you? Most companies have no idea how much money they lose or leave on the table because of poor service. While they have heard that it costs five to six times more to acquire a new customer than to do business with a current or former customer, these businesses have no idea about the flip side of that equation: The cost of poor service.

The following formulas, developed by the United States Office of Consumer Affairs, will help you calculate the cost of providing poor service in your business. To complete the formulas, you need to know three figures:

- ▶ Your annual revenues

- ▶ The number of customers you have

- ▶ The cost of acquiring and keeping those customers (including marketing, advertising, cost of sales, promotions, discounts, etc.)

When you complete the formulas, feel free to use either dollar amounts or percentages. Either way, you will get an eye-opening picture of how expensive poor customer service really is to your business.

What You Lose

Let's assume that your hypothetical business has revenues of $10 million a year from 2,500 customers. Let's also assume that the cost of sales is 66 percent of revenue, or $6.6 million. Now, plug these figures into the formula on page 45 and see what poor customer service really costs your company.

Multiply the total number of customers by 25 percent to get the number of dissatisfied customers. Then, multiply that result by 70 percent, which is an estimate of the number of dissatisfied customers who will stop doing business with you. Divide total annual revenues by the number of customers to get the average revenue of one customer, then multiply this by the number who switched, to get the cost of losing your customers.

Next, calculate your lost opportunity revenue, assuming each dissatisfied customer will tell ten people. Assume that 2 percent of these people will buy elsewhere. Multiply this number by the average revenue per customer and you get your potential lost revenue.

To determine your customer acquisition and replacement costs, multiply your total annual revenues by 66 percent, and divide that number by your total number of customers to get your average cost per customer. Multiply this result by five to get your replacement cost per customer.

Now, add up all your results to get your total cost of poor service. Multiply that figure by 10 to determine the costs of poor service over a 10-year period, considered to be the customer's lifetime for doing business with you.

No business of any size can afford to lose and seek customers continuously. These results should motivate you to improve your customer service programs so that they become customer retention programs.

THE COST OF POOR SERVICE

Lost Customer Revenue

A	Annual revenue	$	10,000,000
B.	Total number of customers		2,500
C.	Percentage of dissatisfied customers	×	.25
D.	Number of dissatisfied customers (C × B)	=	625
E.	Percentage of dissatisfied customers who are likely to switch or stop doing business	×	.70
F.	Number of dissatisfied customers who will switch (D × E)	=	437.5
G.	Average revenue per customer (A ÷ B)	$	4,000
H.	Revenue lost through poor service (F × G)	$	(1,750,000)

Lost Opportunity Revenue

I.	Number of other people dissatisfied customers tell (F × 10)		4,375
J.	Number of potential customers who buy elsewhere due to negative word of mouth (assume one in 50 tell, therefore 1 × I × .02)		87.5
K.	Potential lost revenue (J × G)	$	(350,000)

Customer Replacement Costs

L.	Customer acquisition costs (66% × A)	$	6,600,000
M.	Average cost per customer (L ÷ B)		2,640
N.	Replacement cost for lost customers (M × 5)	$	(13,200)

Total Costs

O.	Total annual cost (H + K + N)	$	(2,113,200)
P.	Total cost over customer's lifetime of doing business for 10 years (O × 10)	$	(21,132,000)

As you can see from this frightening example, this hypothetical company will lose more than $2 million a year due to poor service and customer retention.

Your Turn   *Fill in the same chart for your company. Your results will probably motivate you to improve your customer service and retention efforts.*

THE COST OF POOR SERVICE

Lost Customer Revenue

A. Annual revenue $ _____

B. Total number of customers _____

C. Percentage of dissatisfied customers × .25

D. Number of dissatisfied customers (C × B) = _____

E. Percentage of dissatisfied customers who are likely to switch × .70
or stop doing business _____

F. Number of dissatisfied customers who will switch (D × E) = _____

G. Average revenue per customer (A ÷ B) $ _____

H. Revenue lost through poor service (F × G) $ _____

Lost Opportunity Revenue

I. Number of other people dissatisfied customers tell (F × 10) _____

J. Number of potential customers who buy elsewhere due to negative _____
word of mouth (assume one in 50 tell, therefore 1 × I × .02)

K. Potential lost revenue (J x G) $ _____

Customer Replacement Costs

L. Customer acquisition costs (____ % × A) $ _____

M. Average cost per customer (L ÷ B) $ _____

N. Replacement cost for lost customers (M × 5) $ _____

Total Costs

O. Total annual cost (H + K + N) $ _____

P. Total cost over customer's lifetime of doing business for $ _____
10 years (O × 10)

The Cost of Poor Quality

Calculating the cost of poor quality is slightly more difficult than determining the cost of poor service, although arguments can be made that the same formula could be used. After all, if you provide a poor quality product or service, you will lose current customers and potential future customers.

You need to consider some other things when you determine the cost of quality in your organization. Four factors that you can put a price on to identify your cost of poor quality are:

1. **Performance Cost**—The cost of doing it right the first time. This is the cost associated with producing something that is error-free and that will not have to be redone or reworked.

2. **Rework or Failure Cost**—The cost of doing something over again. Repair, rework and correcting failures can account for up to 50 percent of your cost of doing business. Another item that must be included in this factor is the cost of making restitution or amends to a customer.

3. **Detection Costs**—The cost of detecting or finding quality problems. These include inspection costs, salaries, and any other extra procedures that contribute to detecting problems before they go out the door.

4. **Prevention Costs**—The cost of identifying quality impairments before they reach what is normally called the quality inspection or quality control stage. Prevention costs are minimized when every worker is capable of inspecting his or her own work. These costs can also be hidden in the detection cost factor.

Be sure you investigate these four factors to determine your cost of poor quality.

Quality itself never ultimately costs, it pays. Determine how much it will pay you to provide quality products and services by checking your position in these five key areas:

1. **Price**—Higher quality and better service allows you to charge more for your goods and services. Research supports this position.

2. **Profitability**—True quality, which is preventing errors by doing it right the first time according to expectations established by customers, leads to cost savings and increased sales. The result, especially when combined with higher prices, is increased profitability.

3. **Market Share**—Research again supports the position that higher quality means greater market share. Even if you are charging more for your products or services, people are willing to pay the price simply because they know they are getting quality and value for their money.

4. **Cost**—Improved quality decreases production costs because you are only doing something once. Poor quality increases production costs because you always have to do it over again or make reparations to your customers in hopes of keeping them.

5. **Marketing and Advertising**—The relative costs here will decrease for two reasons. The first is that you will be selling more, so your effective cost per sale will decrease even if you increase your advertising expenditures. The second is that your word-of-mouth marketing and referral business will increase, thereby lowering your external advertising costs.

Another thing you must consider about the cost of poor quality is your customer's cost for doing business with you. How much time, effort and money must a customer expend to make the first purchase from you, and then come back and get the product repaired or replaced? These costs must also be figured into your calculations.

When you combine all the factors related to the cost of poor customer service and the cost of poor quality, you begin to realize how important it is to provide the best of both. The dollars you can lose are enormous, and they cannot be made up through cost-cutting measures and expense cost containment. It is a rare company that can improve customer service and quality by cutting costs. However, most companies that improve customer service and quality also realize a cost savings and an increase in profitability.

Another approach to calculating the cost of poor service is to determine how many customers you lose on an annual basis, and multiply that number by their average revenue value to your company. Then, multiply the amount by your expected or realized profit margin for the year. Add in other costs such as account closing costs, expenses related to attempted recovery such as salaries and overhead, and, again, lost opportunity revenue.

Here is an example of the cost of losing customers for one company.

Number of Lost Accounts Annually	1000
Average Revenue per Account	× $1000.00
Total Lost Annual Revenues	**$1,000,000.00**
Lost Profits (assume 10% profit margin)	× .10
Total Lost Profits	**$100,000.00**
Closing and Recovery Costs per Account	$50.00
Number of Lost Accounts (again)	× 1000
Total Closing and Recovery Costs	**$50,000.00**
TOTAL COSTS OF LOST ACCOUNTS	**$150,000.00**
TOTAL COSTS OF POOR SERVICE	**$1,150,000.00**

LIFETIME VALUE OF A CUSTOMER

Most business owners know that it costs to get a customer, and it also costs when the business loses a customer.

Two important figures for you to know are the cost of acquiring a customer and what that customer's lifetime value is to your business. Knowing that it costs five or six times as much to acquire a new customer as it does to continue doing business with a current or former customer, multiply your lost revenue per customer by five. While the value may not be totally realistic or 100 percent accurate, it gives you an idea of how much money you may be spending to get a new customer into your business.

Another way to do this is to carefully track all expenditures for marketing, advertising and promotion. Divide that figure by the number of new customers each activity generates. This gives you a more accurate picture of your acquisition costs and enables you to calculate the lifetime value of your customer, as well as your typical customer's marginal net worth—the amount you can actually spend to acquire a customer, based on the profit you expect to make from repeat purchases during his or her lifetime with you.

These concepts are powerful customer service and marketing tools. Companies have experienced exponential growth from their understanding and use of this single concept. Your understanding of the lifetime value/marginal net worth concept can help you grow your business faster than your competitors.

Lifetime Value and Marginal Net Worth

Most companies allocate a certain dollar amount or a fixed percentage of revenues to marketing and advertising. They do this because "it's always been done this way." Many Fortune 500 companies create their marketing budgets this way, even though it is one of the least effective ways to determine how much money should be spent on customer acquisition. Most of your competitors are probably doing it, as well.

Here is an alternative which will leave your competitors wondering what happened as you outmarket and outservice them and grow your business. Let's say that you track all your marketing expenditures and determine that it costs you $100 to acquire one new customer. This amount may be a lot or a little for your particular business. It is just used here as an example.

You determine that each customer you acquire spends $500 with you on their first purchase. Your gross profit is $400, which is the $500 in revenue minus the cost to acquire that customer. Subtract another 20 percent, or $100, for overhead, which leaves your net profit as $300 per customer.

Your data show that each customer makes four purchases from you a year, and that your average satisfied customer stays with you for five years. Using five years as the lifetime of the customer, the lifetime value to you is $10,000 in gross revenue ($500 * 4 purchases * 5 yrs). And, you make an additional $100 on each purchase, because there are no new acquisition costs. As you can see, you are already making money.

Knowing this, you can decide how much more you are willing to spend to acquire a new customer. Previously, you spent $100 to get a new customer; you can easily spend $300 (your net profit from the first sale and their initial marginal net worth) or even $500 (your gross revenue from the first sale) to get that customer, since this customer will be worth $10,000 to you over five years—and most of it will be pure profit.

There is one caveat to this concept. You must provide superior customer service to each and every customer to ensure that they keep coming back to you for those five years—or more. If your service does not meet and exceed their expectations, you can be sure that they will take their business elsewhere.

Now you have a little-known secret in your marketing and customer service arsenal to grow your business. I can assure you that maybe one in 100 or even 1,000 business owners has any idea what this concept is and how it works. Since you are now that one, think about how quickly and successfully you will grow your business. Just remember to provide great customer service.

Using the concept of lifetime value and marginal net worth forces you to combine marketing with great customer service to get and keep customers for life. And, you get another benefit. Customers who stay with you a long time tend to refer more people to you, which decreases your customer acquisition costs even more. This leaves you additional monies to go out and acquire new customers.

TEN REASONS FOR POOR SERVICE

Think of yourself as a customer for a moment. Do you remember the great service you received from a business or the poor service? If you are like most people, you can relate more service horror stories than positive experiences. Since that's the case for most people, it is probably also true for your customers.

What are some of the reasons you would give for not doing business with a company? Do your customers have similar reasons for not coming back to you? Seriously consider the reasons you may lose a customer.

The following list is compiled from various sources, including research with my clients as to why people receive poor service. It is astonishing to realize that customers want to give someone money for a product or service, and business owners (or their employees) do everything possible to turn those customers off. It does not make sense, especially when customers are the lifeblood of any business.

You are in business to get, satisfy and keep customers. If you do these things, your business will grow and prosper.

 *Your Turn*

Read this list of ten reasons companies provide poor service. When you are done, read them again.

1. The company does not have a customer service philosophy.

2. Complaints are handled and resolved poorly.

3. Employees are poorly trained.

4. Employees have uncaring or negative attitudes.

5. Employees are treated poorly.

6. Employees are not empowered to provide good service, to take responsibility, and to make decisions that will satisfy customers.

7. Differences in perception between what businesses think customers want and what customers actually want.

8. Differences in perception between the product or service businesses think they provide and what customers think they receive.

9. Differences in perception between the way businesses think customers want to be treated and the way customers really want to be treated, or are actually treated.

10. Differences in perception between the value a business thinks it provides and the value a customer believes he or she receives.

Answer the following questions:

► How many of these reasons have you experienced?

► How many are happening in your business right now?

► What can you do about it, so that you can keep, rather than lose, customers?

Read the list again. Did you notice four of the reasons have to do with how employees are treated and trained by the company, and another four have to do with differences in perceptions between customers and the business? You might say that the first two reasons also relate to the employees. And, all the reasons reflect on management or ownership.

How will you remedy any or all of these situations if they occur in your business today? Remember that people are loyal to businesses because they feel they are treated well, they receive good value for their money, and they are psychologically or physically attached to the business.

Do everything possible to make certain that your customers do not want to switch to your competitors. In many cases, it is more important for you to make the psychological switching costs to the customer "expensive and painful"; if you provide a great service, most customers will feel they cannot afford to go to your competitors.

SETTING UP CUSTOMER SERVICE SYSTEMS IN YOUR BUSINESS

Has this ever happened to you? You purchase something, then have a problem with it. You go back to the store to either return it or get it fixed. You tell your story to the person behind the counter, who tells you nothing can be done about it, and you need to talk with the owner, manager or the customer service department. None of them is available.

Perhaps you call a company and tell your situation to someone on the phone who, after patiently listening, tells you she cannot help you. She transfers you to someone who should be able to help. You tell your story again, only to find that person cannot help you either. You start to get frustrated. You are transferred a third time, and this time you get voice mail. Now you are really steamed. You vow never to do business with the company again.

In today's business climate, with well-educated and sophisticated customers and increasing competition, it is hard to believe that any business would not have readily accessible customer service systems in place. However, I continue to find many businesses who make it hard for the customer.

Many business owners are trying to improve their customer service. They would tell you that they are doing everything possible to serve and satisfy their customers. Yet, when you try to get some service, it is either poor or nonexistent.

So, what are you supposed to do? The answer is very simple. You need to set up customer service systems and processes in your businesses that welcome customers, that make it easy for them to do business with you, and that help them get their problems resolved and questions answered, as quickly as possible, to the customers' satisfaction.

Establishing customer service systems takes a great deal of work. Companies have to invest time and money into the process. But, it does not have to be difficult. You can actually establish these protocols very easily, as long as you are willing to invest the time and energy. And, you have to get your employees behind the movement if you want it to succeed.

SEVEN STEPS TO A CUSTOMER SERVICE SYSTEM

I have broken down the development of a customer service system in a company to a simple seven step process. Regardless of whether you are a one person business or you have any number of employees, follow these seven steps and you will be a successful service provider. You do not have to follow these steps in any specific order, although the sequence I present them in will get you the best and the quickest results.

Step 1: Total Management Commitment

Customer service programs only succeed when there is total management commitment. This commitment must begin at the top. The president, CEO, chairman of the board or owner must develop and communicate a clear vision of what the service quality system is going to be, how it is going to be implemented, what the staff should expect when implementing it, how it will be used to satisfy and retain customers, and how it will be supported over time. Everyone in the company must do more than just pay lip service to customer service. Management must model the behavior they want employees to perform—walk the talk. They must also treat employees as well as they want employees to treat customers. Everyone must work together to deliver superior customer service.

Step 2: Know Your Customers (Intimately)

Do everything possible to get to know your customers intimately and to understand them totally. Some people suggest that you get to know your customers better than they know themselves. This means knowing what they like and dislike about your business; changes they may want you to make; their current and future needs, wants and expectations; what motivates them to buy or change suppliers; what you must do to satisfy them, retain them and make them loyal.

You learn all this by simply asking your customers. When you have learned about your customers and you think you know them as well as you know yourself, learn about them all over again. Their needs change daily—even hourly—and you must know how to satisfy those needs. Their requirements and expectations change also, and you must be able to meet and exceed those expectations.

Knowing your customers intimately, and on an ongoing basis requires that you keep in constant contact with them. Call them regularly. Write to them. Invite them to lunch or to your office or facility. Find out exactly what they are doing, what they need, and what they want you to do for them. This constant contact helps you develop the retention and loyalty you need, because they know you are interested in them.

Step 3: Develop Standards of Service Quality Performance

Customer service appears to be an intangible item because it is based on perception. However, it does have tangible and visible aspects that you can manage and measure.

For example, customers dislike waiting for the telephone to be answered or being placed on hold for long periods of time. How many rings does it take for your phone to be answered, and how long do you place your customers on hold without getting back to them to tell them what is going on? How many transfers or how many steps through an automatic call-distribution menu does it take for a customer to get a question answered or a complaint resolved? How long does it take to process and ship an order? Is it shipped correctly the first time? What is your policy on customer returns, refunds, exchanges and complaints?

These are all tangible aspects of customer service, and they can be measured. If you have any doubts about what to measure, just ask your customers. They will tell you (perhaps not directly or exactly) what they are looking for and how they judge service quality. Since service quality and satisfaction only exist in the minds of the customers, you must develop your standards and measurement systems to meet and exceed their perceptions.

Step 4: Hire, Train and Compensate Good Staff

Superior customer service performance that results in customer satisfaction and retention can only be provided by competent, qualified people. Your service quality is only as good as the people who deliver it. If you want your business to be good to people—and that is a requirement for success in today's business environment—you must hire good people.

Once you hire your employees, train them extensively to provide superior customer service and do things right the first time. Be sure they understand your company's standards of service quality performance and the customer's expectations of service quality. Train them in their own jobs and train them in other jobs as well. Let them experience being a customer of your company; have them make suggestions for improving the treatment of customers.

Once they are trained, compensate them well. Remember the costs associated with losing a customer and acquiring new ones? The same formulas hold true for recruiting, hiring and training new staff. Acquisition costs can be staggering. Train them well and compensate them well. After all, they are your company's initial contact with the buying public. Your employees are your company in the eyes and ears of your customers. If they give bad service, your customers perceive your entire company as giving bad service. And remember, the higher your standards of performance, the better your employees will perform.

Finally, empower your people to make decisions and do the right thing to satisfy your customers. This concept is called empowerment and enablement. The staff should not have to look for you or a manager every time a customer asks a question, has a return or a complaint or needs a problem solved. There are legions of stories about empowered employees who made decisions that were against company policy but that satisfied and retained a customer, with the end-result of both the business and the customer winning. If you are going to place people in customer-contact positions, give them the authority that goes with this tremendous responsibility. They must be able to do whatever it takes to satisfy the customer.

Step 5: Reward Service Quality Accomplishments

Always recognize, reward and reinforce superior service performances. Do this for your employees and for your customers. Provide psychological, and sometimes financial, incentives for your people. Help them motivate themselves to do even better. Broadcast and make a big deal about all types of service accomplishments that result in more satisfied customers. Recognize and reward even the small wins in a manner similar to what you would use for the major accomplishments.

Also, reward your customers for good customer behavior. Everyone wants to be appreciated and to feel important—especially your customers. Provide them with recognition and appreciation, just as you would your employees. They will be motivated to refer more business to you and to be more loyal to you. In both cases, employee and customer turnover decreases while loyalty and commitment increase.

Step 6: Stay Close To Your Customers

Even when you have gotten to know your customers intimately (Step 2), you must do everything possible to stay close to them. Keep in touch in any and every way possible. Invite them for site visits. Go visit them. Send them letters, cards, newsletters, and published articles of interest to them. Conduct continuous research to learn about their changing needs and expectations.

Ask them questions right after they make a purchase. When they do not buy, ask them why they did not make a purchase. Mail them questionnaires and other types of surveys. Call and ask them how you can do a better job for them. Get them involved in your business on customer councils, advisory boards, focus groups, and job swapping. Do whatever it takes to stay close to your customers and continue to build and maintain this valuable relationship. Consider using a database program or a contact management program to track the information you gather.

Your relationship with a customer really solidifies after he or she makes a purchase. Let customers know you care about them and that you will support their purchases. Make sure they are satisfied, and find out what you must do to maintain that satisfaction and loyalty. Do everything in your power to keep your name in their minds and to keep their perception of your service quality at the highest level possible.

Step 7: Work Toward Continuous Improvement

"If it ain't broke, break it." You cannot rest, even when you have friendly and accessible customer service systems, have hired and trained the best people for the job, and have learned everything you can about your customers. No system or program is perfect—least of all customer service and satisfaction—because they are based on a person's perceptions. Therefore, you must continually work to improve your customer service and performance quality.

Customers who are initially satisfied with their purchases will perceive your attempts at continuous service quality improvement as very positive. Many will even want to help. Welcome them with open arms. They are your best source of information about how to get better in their eyes and minds. When you implement their recommendations and suggestions, they perceive that you value them even more, and will do even more business with you. The result will be more satisfied customers, a happier staff and greater profits.

The Customer's Perspective

These seven steps will help you develop a customer service system for your business. The key is to develop this system from the customer's perspective. It should be easy for the customer to access and use; everything done within the system should be done to satisfy the customer. Do not set up the system to make it easier for your staff to provide service—your staff may even have to work a little harder to make it easier for the customer. The results will be more satisfied customers and more business.

Customer service pays, it does not cost. Your only goal for being in business is to acquire, serve, satisfy and keep customers. Work to provide the best possible customer service, as defined by your customers, and you will have the most loyal and satisfied customers in your industry. When this occurs, the growth, expansion and increased profitability of your business will take care of themselves.

ASK YOURSELF

► How do you show that either the "customer is always right" or the "customer is always the customer" in your business?

► What does it cost you to acquire and lose a customer?

► Which of the seven steps to establishing an excellent customer service system are already in place in your business?

► Which steps do you plan to implement immediately? Describe how you will do this.

CHAPTER FOUR

MAKING CUSTOMER SERVICE WORK

UNDER-PROMISE AND OVER-DELIVER

Are you aware of what will happen if you overpromise something and underdeliver it? Do it once and customers have a hard time believing anything else you say. If anything, you must underpromise and overdeliver. Let's look at an example.

Several years ago, a very large cable television company promoted its new customer service program and policy with a program they called The Customer First. Their policy was to do whatever it took to satisfy the customer. At least, that is what their ads promised. They ran a big marketing campaign to inform subscribers about the great service they would now receive. According to their ads, staff members were trained in the most important customer service skills and they were ready and waiting to serve customers.

As a customer, I called the main office and asked to speak with whomever was in charge of the training program. The first person I spoke with said she knew nothing about a program by that name. When I told her it was advertised on TV, she said she never saw the commercial.

STRIKE ONE!

She transferred me to a supervisor in the office who said he knew about the program and knew they were advertising it. He did not know who was in charge of it. When I asked if he had ever gone through the training program, he said, "No," and added he was not aware of any training classes that were scheduled.

STRIKE TWO!

I needed to add another cable outlet in my son's room, so I called the company and scheduled an installer. He arrived two hours late, dirty and sweaty from a previous job. He made no apologies for his lateness or appearance. Before he began his installation, I asked him to hide the cable under the carpet and run it through the closet. He said, "No problem," and proceeded with his installation. When he finished, he told me the television was working and I would need to pick up a box from the office. I thanked him and he left.

When I checked the installation, I found that the cable wire was on the floor, not run through the closet as I had asked, and it was not even tacked down. I called the cable company and told the installation supervisor what happened. He explained that the installer was a subcontractor and so the cable company could not be responsible for his behavior, appearance or performance.

STRIKES THREE, FOUR and FIVE!

I told the supervisor to send someone out to my house the next day to do something about the wires in my house, and that he clearly is responsible for subcontractors. I explained that if the problem was not taken care of immediately and to my satisfaction, I would contact the media and tell them about the false advertising the cable company was doing. The next day, the supervisor came out to my house, fixed the wiring and hooked up my cable box himself, and apologized for the problems. I appreciated his attempt at service recovery and I told him so, but it was not enough. When he left he still insisted that his company was not responsible for subcontractors, even though I told him that anyone he sends out on a job for his company is his company in the eyes and minds of the customers. He just did not see it that way.

STRIKE SIX, YOU'RE OUT!

Obviously, this company (and many others) had not trained their employees in how to make customer service work. This is not a unique occurrence.

Your Turn

Answer the following question:

► In your experience, what are some of the industries and companies that have advertised superior customer service and have not delivered?

Here is part of my list, based on my personal experiences:

- ► Car dealerships
- ► Gas stations
- ► Plumbers
- ► Electricians
- ► Cable TV
- ► Restaurants
- ► Clothing stores
- ► Music stores

I am not saying that every business in every industry I have mentioned or that is on your list does not deliver on customer service promises—I am saying that certain companies do not deliver.

THE SKILLS OF EXCELLENT CUSTOMER SERVICE

Every company can provide great customer service to each and every one of its customers all the time. This requires ongoing training in a specific set of skills, along with the empowerment and enablement concepts discussed earlier.

The training is more than smile training. Only a few years ago, companies began training their employees to provide superior customer service by smiling. That was it. The idea was that if you smiled at customers and nodded in agreement, they would believe you were providing superior service. It did not take long before businesses realized that smiling alone was not enough for employees to provide great customer service. Other skills were needed.

Through my research and consulting, I have identified seven primary skills that employees need to develop to provide excellent customer service:

Skill 1: *Building Rapport*

Skill 2: *Interpersonal Communication*

Skill 3: *Effective Listening*

Skill 4: *Telephone Courtesy*

Skill 5: *Handling Angry Customers (and Problem Solving)*

Skill 6: *Complaint Management (and Problem Solving)*

These skills help people deliver excellent customer service. Many people say that building rapport, communication and listening are part and parcel of the same skill set. While they can all come under the heading of communication, they are separate and distinct skills that must be addressed individually.

Success in customer service is based on a system-wide approach to skill building; I strongly recommend that you provide training for your staff in each. This means that all of the skills must be trained and practiced for effective performance. In this chapter, you will see how each of these skills affects quality customer service.

Skill 1: Building Rapport

Building rapport is essential for a successful customer inter-action. Rapport leads to credibility and trust, liking and friendliness, and a feeling of comfort.

Think back to a situation where you were with someone who made you feel uncomfortable. Your body probably became tense, you did not think as clearly as you normally would, and you just knew things were not right. Your greatest hope may have been to find a way out of the situation.

Now, think of someone that you get along with very well—you are very comfortable together, as if you both know what the other is going to say before it is said. You seem to know what the other person is thinking or feeling. You just "click." The reason for these positive things is that you are in rapport.

Since you and your customers both want to feel good, you want to be in rapport with them. How do you develop this rapport, and how do you do it rapidly in a service situation?

If you follow this sequence of actions, you will find yourself able to develop rapport with customers and everyone else, almost instantly.

As a customer approaches you (or you approach a customer), notice everything you can about that person—their appearance, their clothes, their cologne or perfume, their hair color, their jewelry. Greet the customer with a smile and an enthusiastic hello. If possible, learn the customer's name and use it several times. Say something nice about the customer, especially regarding his or her appearance (or anything else). Pay attention to the customer's posture and body language and begin to mirror that: Stand as they do or fold your arms as they do. Just make sure your body language and posture is perceived as similar to theirs. When the customer speaks, notice the rate and pitch of the speech. When it is your turn to talk, mirror their speech patterns as closely as possible, without mimicking them. And, when they speak, listen attentively.

While this may seem like a lot for you to do, it actually can occur within the first fifteen or thirty seconds of every customer encounter. That is really all the time you need to establish rapport. All you have to do is smile, greet them enthusiastically, learn their name, mirror their body language and speech patterns, and listen attentively. It should take you no time at all. When these skills become a habit for you and they occur naturally, you will not even be aware of any energy being expended to build rapport with your customers. And, customers will love you for it, even if they cannot explain it.

Skill 2: Interpersonal Communication

This section identifies some of the most important interpersonal communication skills you must develop in order to provide superior customer service. You can use these skills in all aspects of your service encounters, and they will help you improve all your relationships.

First, decide on your communication stance with regard to customers. Will you take the "resist stance" or the "assist stance?" While the choice may seem obvious, some businesses still believe they could do a great job if only the customers would not get in the way. I recommend you take the assist stance. Once you do this, be aware that effective communication is only defined by the response you receive.

If you ask a customer to go to register A to pay for a purchase, and they go to register B, they obviously did not understand your instructions. Even if they understood what you said, their behavior in response to your instructions made your communication ineffective. That is why it is imperative for you as an effective communicator to simultaneously be aware of the effect you want from your communication and the response you actually receive.

When you do not get the desired effect, you—not the customer or employee—need to change your words, your behavior or your communication approach. It is always best for you as the service provider to adapt to the customer, rather than the other way around.

I have identified Ten Key Elements to Effective Communication:

1. **Paying Attention**—This means giving the speaker your undivided attention.

2. **Adaptability/Flexibility**—This is your readiness and ability to change what you are doing to improve communication.

3. **Eye Contact**—You must look at people when you communicate with them.

4. **Asking Questions**—The best way to learn something is to ask about it.

5. **Listening**—No one ever learned anything by talking. Listen twice as much as you speak.

6. **Stories/Analogies/Metaphors**—People communicate more effectively and remember more of what is communicated when they use these indirect methods, rather than simply stating facts.

7. **Mirroring**—When you match another person's body language and speech patterns as closely as possible without mimicking them, they perceive that you are like them and they start to like and trust you immediately.

8. **Rapport**—You have to build trust as quickly as possible to open the lines of communication.

9. **Pacing/Leading**—These two techniques develop an effective communication. With pacing, you follow the other person's lead. When you lead, they match what you do.

10. **Responding**—This involves knowing when to respond and what to say. Sometimes, your non-verbal responses say more than your verbal/vocal responses.

Study these ten keys to effective communication. They will definitely help you work better with employees and customers.

Your Turn

Answer the following questions:

▶ Which of these ten keys do you use regularly?

▶ Which of these ten keys do you need to develop?

Most of the people who succeed in life are effective communicators. And, when you think about almost every customer service encounter, its major component is communication between two or more people.

Unfortunately, some service providers do not possess these skills and refuse to develop them. You have probably run into these people. They seem to go out of their way to miscommunicate, rather than communicate with you and other customers. Here are ten things that people do to enhance miscommunication.

Ten Ways to Miscommunicate with a Customer

1. **Explaining too soon**—You begin to justify yourself before the customer finishes saying everything he/she wants to say.

2. **Interpreting**—You get into the reasons behind the customer's communication and respond to that instead of the content of the message.

3. **Punishing or Retaliating**—You want to get even with a customer or get back at a customer because you think you heard something that was bothersome.

4. **Pretending not to understand the message**—Most of the time people are clear in getting their message across, but sometimes the listener pretends to have difficulty grasping or understanding the impact of what is being said. Not getting the point can take the wind out of the sails of a customer, especially if you do it intentionally.

5. **Passing the buck**—This response to a customer's communication (complaint or request) means you fail to accept responsibility for your actions. A common tactic in passing the buck is to attempt to put the responsibility back on the customer or on someone else.

6. **Changing the subject**—Different methods get the customer off his or her communication track. You might suddenly suggest an entirely different topic. You might shift from a feeling-level conversation to an intellectual discussion. You might reply specifically to the content of the communication, rather than to the underlying emotion. The result of any of these strategies is that the customer feels he/she has not been taken seriously.

7. **Turning the communication into a joke**—You crack a joke or make a sarcastic remark when the customer is being very serious. When you get caught you say, "I was only kidding when I said that. I didn't expect you to take me seriously." You might also make light of a customer's concerns or complaints, leaving him or her feeling that none of what they said was taken seriously.

8. **Not responding**—As a general rule in communication, any response is better than no response. Possibly the most frustrating response of all is to get nothing back.

9. **Condescending**— Communication occurs most effectively between equals or approximate equals. One way to impede communication is to pull rank or to remind the customer of your status as the service provider. The person who resorts to one-upmanship is distancing himself/herself in the interaction.

10. **Being busy, bored or absent-minded**—The customer who is communicating with you usually expects to be taken seriously and to be given attention and time enough to say what he/she wants to say. Imagine the effect on the customer of being told by you, "Sorry, I didn't hear you. My mind was on something else. Would you repeat what you said to me?" It is equally distressing for a customer to try to talk to you on the run about an important topic because you do not have the time to sit down with them. Make the time.

If you need a reminder on how to communicate effectively with customers, think of how you feel when a service provider does one of these things to you.

If you are doing any of these now, stop and begin working to improve. Go back and re-read the Ten Key Elements to Effective Communication. To be successful, you must develop these interpersonal communication skills.

Skill 3: Effective Listening

By now, it must be clear that the way to find out exactly what your customers need, want and expect from you is to ask them. Once you ask them, it is essential that you listen carefully to their responses.

All too often, people ask questions and do not wait for or listen to the answer. You probably know a few people like that too. Does it aggravate and annoy you when they ask you something and then do not have the courtesy to allow you time to completely answer their questions? Your customers feel the same way you do.

It is vitally important that you listen to all your customers. Everyone has something important to say to you, either personally or in writing. In fact, by listening to your customers you get some of the best free consulting advice anywhere. Their comments and feedback often indicate what you can do to improve your business and sell more.

Over the past twelve years, I have asked over 25,000 people what they expected most in the way of customer service. While everyone listed good value at a fair price, a quality product or service, and good service, the number one thing people wanted from someone they did business with was to be listened to. I have also asked thousands of people what they wanted most from a relationship with another person. Their answer was the same: to be listened to. If you have children, ask them what they want from you as a parent. They will tell you they want you to listen to them more often and more effectively.

That is what customer service is about. You must listen to your customers. Remember that service and selling are all about people and their relationships. During a seminar, a sales professional "insulted" me by saying I was more service-oriented than sales-oriented. I thanked her profusely, because I am a firm believer that your attitude towards service will come across during your sale and people will be more likely to buy from you once, and then again. And, to be customer service oriented, I have to be an effective listener. So do you.

Remember: Listening is a Skill

Hearing is what you are born with. Listening is a skill that is learned and acquired. Listening is what you do with your hearing.

Here are some of the more essential skills and facts you need to know about to become an effective listener.

1. The first thing an effective listener does is *pay attention* to the speaker. That means focusing on who the person is and what they are saying. Give them your undivided attention so that you can clearly hear their message.

2. Then *interpret* their message in light of your own perceptions, experiences, and the context in which the message is sent.

3. This allows you to *evaluate* the message and make a judgment on what it means to you.

4. Then, *provide feedback* to the speaker (or writer) by acknowledging you understand what they were trying to communicate and responding to the message.

Remember that the definition of an effective communication is a speaker-listener interaction where the response is appropriate to the intent of the message that was sent.

You must do these things regardless of the type of listening you are engaged in. There are four types of listening: active, passive, reflective and empathetic.

Active Listening is when you are physically and vocally involved with the speaker. You motivate them to continue speaking by saying things like "yes; I understand," "mm-hmm," "go ahead," "continue," and "go on; right," or by simply nodding your head in agreement or smiling at them as they speak. These are all signs that you are paying attention and you want the speaker to continue.

In a customer service situation, it is imperative that you actively listen. The last thing a customer wants from you as the service provider is for you to be inattentive, have your attention wander, or act as if you are uninterested. The customer should be the center of your world when they are there in front of you. There should be nothing that distracts you unless it is vitally important. Pay attention to the customer and be actively involved with whatever they are speaking about.

If they are asking you questions, the only way you can provide accurate answers is to listen. If they are complaining about something, the only way you can resolve their complaint is to listen. If they are just making conversation, the only way you can make them feel comfortable is to listen. When they are comfortable with you, they trust you more. When they trust you more, they buy more from you. And, when customers are comfortable with a service provider, they will allow that person more leeway in case a mistake is made. And, since we are all human, we all make mistakes from time to time.

The listening skill you do not want to evidence in front of a customer is called **passive listening**. With passive listening, you listen, but you do not show any signs of life. You are just there. You hear everything that is being said. You take it in, evaluate it and formulate your response. But, you do not give any indication that you are involved with what the customer says. The customer gets turned off because he or she does not know what you think.

If passive listening is your preferred style, I suggest you change it immediately if you want to be able to provide superior customer service. Practice your active listening skills on family and friends and ask them for honest feedback. Work hard to improve this aspect of your behavioral repertoire and you will find that your business will improve.

Many people whom others call great conversationalists are actually great listeners. Try this at your next social function. During a conversation, ask the person or people you are speaking with some questions about themselves. When they respond, actively listen to them. Invite them to continue speaking by saying things like "That's interesting. Tell me more." The more you do this with more people, the more people will begin to call you a great conversationalist.

After you develop your active listening skills and get rid of your passive listening skills, you move on to "higher order" listening skills. The first of these is **reflective listening.**

In reflective listening, you actively listen to the speaker, motivate them to continue their part of the conversation, and when they take a break, verbally "reflect" what they have said by repeating it back to them or paraphrasing it. This action on your part invites them to expand on that particular topic and to continue speaking. Reflective listening is a skill that many therapists use to keep their clients talking. You will do well to develop this skill to improve your customer service.

Here is an example of using active and reflective listening in a customer service situation:

CUSTOMER: I bought this dress here and it fits really well. I really like it but when I tried it on at home, it didn't match anything else I had. (*customer takes a breath*)

SALESPERSON: Yes, I see.

CUSTOMER: I tried to find something to go with it, but I just can't seem to find anything. And, I'm not sure if my husband wants me to keep the dress. But I really do like it. (*breath*)

SALESPERSON (*reflective listening*): So, you really like the dress and it fits well, but you can't seem to find anything that goes with it and you're not sure if your husband wants you to keep it. Is there anything else?

Now, the conversation can continue. The salesperson responds both actively and reflectively to the customer. When you have this skill down pat, you can move to **empathic listening.**

Empathic listening is when you communicate to the customer that you truly understand their situation. Some phrases that show empathy are "I understand" and "I know." If you say "I know exactly how you feel," you had better know exactly how they feel. If you do not, the customer will respond to you with something like "How could you know exactly how I feel? Did this ever happen to you?" And, if it did not, you really cannot know exactly how they feel. So, while empathy is the highest order listening skill you can have, temper it by being careful with your words.

In the years that I have done customer service training and consulting, I have found people universally want to be understood when they speak. Even if you disagree with what they are saying, or the customer is completely wrong, show empathy first by making it clear that you understand their feelings, where they are coming from, and what they are thinking—before you state your side of the discussion.

You want to get all the way to empathic with your customers so they can develop a feeling of rapport and trust with you. The more comfortable they feel around you, the more business they will do with you. Pay attention to them and listen to them.

Your Turn

Answer the following questions:

▶ Which of the following ten things that can influence your listening to a customer can you control?

▶ Which ones can you control your reactions to?

▶ Which ones don't you care about or pay attention to? (**Hint:** *They are all extremely important.*)

1. Who the customer is: Is he or she a regular customer? A big spender? A friend?

2. The customer's speaking style: Is it fast or slow; to the point or dragged out?

3. The customer's appearance: Well dressed or shabby? Clean or dirty?

4. Your past experiences with this customer: Good or bad? Friendly or unfriendly?

5. Your mood: Good or bad? Happy or sad? Friendly or unfriendly?

6. Your health: How do you feel? Are you taking care of yourself?

7. The time and place of the conversation: Your office/ store or the customer's? Day/night?

8. The setting or the situation: Calm or tense? Inside or outside? Hot or cold?

9. The perceived power of the customer: Does their business have a major impact on yours?

10. The importance to you of what the customer is saying: Is it meaningful for you?

These ten things have a tremendous influence on your ability to listen to a customer. Any one of them that becomes negative can cause you to miss something important that the customer is saying. It may seem like a lot of things to worry about just to be an effective listener but, as you develop your listening skills, these things will begin to fall into place naturally.

The chart on page 79, Ten Characteristics of Poor and Good Listeners, identifies differences between poor and good listeners. It gives you an idea of what you might do and what you must do to improve your listening skills.

Think back to any customer service situation in your experience. Was there a time when you spoke with a customer and you did all of the following, and the situation was handled to the customer's total and complete satisfaction? Did you . . .

► Refrain from interrupting the customer?

► Do everything possible to put the customer at ease?

► Concentrate on what the customer was saying?

► Remove all possible distractions while you listened?

- ▶ Show empathy for the customer's situation?

- ▶ Pay attention to what was being said as well as the non-verbal cues to find the real meaning of the customer's message?

- ▶ Control your emotions, especially if you disagreed with something the customer said?

- ▶ Refrain from making any judgments before you heard all the details?

- ▶ Ask questions to get more information, to keep the customer talking, and to help you better understand the customer's situation?

- ▶ Provide feedback to the customer to show you understood exactly what was being said?

Undoubtedly, you have had many customer service situations when you could answer "yes" to all these questions. You did it then without thinking about it—you can do it now constantly.

It is imperative for the success of any interpersonal relationship that the people involved be able to communicate. While it is very important to speak properly and clearly, and to say what you mean, it is just as important to listen actively and empathically, to provide feedback and to acknowledge that you understand what the customer is saying. To provide great customer service, you need to be a good listener. Then, you can move on in the relationship to other things.

Ten Characteristics of Poor and Good Listeners

Poor Listeners	Good Listeners
1. Call the subject uninteresting.	1. Find every message useful and interesting.
2. Criticize the speaker's delivery.	2. Focus on the message.
3. Interrupt.	3. Hear the speaker out.
4. Listen only for facts, and all of them.	4. Listen for central ideas.
5. Divide or fake their attention.	5. Pay close attention.
6. Think more about what they are going to say than what the speaker is saying.	6. Wait until the speaker finishes before thinking about their response.
7. Create and/or tolerate distractions.	7. Eliminates and removes distractions.
8. Tune out difficult material.	8. Challenge themselves with difficult material.
9. Get emotional or let emotional words block the message.	9. Are aware of their emotional reactions to words.
10. Waste the time between thought-speed (10,000 + WPM) and speech-speed (150–250 WPM).	10. Find every message useful and interesting.

Skill 4: Telephone Courtesy

When it comes to customer service, the telephone is the heart and soul of any small business. People call you to find out where you are located, to check on inventory and pricing, to learn your hours of operation, to ask questions, to register complaints, and just to talk. Much of your success is dependent on how well you and your employees handle the phone. This may seem very simple to you and that telephone skills should be obvious. However, have you ever had these things happen to you?

► You call a company and the phone rings and rings and no one picks up, not even an answering machine.

► You call a company and an automatic call distribution system picks up and tells you your options. When you press your option, nobody personally answers the call.

► You call someplace and they answer the phone with "Yeah, whaddaya want?"

► You call a business and they answer "Who's this?"

Your Turn

Answer the following questions:

► Have you ever called your own business to determine how well they answer the phone?

► Have you ever had someone else call your business and go through a problem scenario to see how well your staff handles the situation on the phone?

If you have never done these, you should. You will gain a world of insight into the effect the phone is having on your business.

The Beginnings of Superior Telephone Customer Service

Great service begins when the phone rings. Every time that phone rings, you have an opportunity to make a sale. It does not matter if the caller is a current customer, a former customer or a prospective customer. Whoever is calling is doing so for a reason; you or your staff can create the right or the wrong atmosphere just in the way you handle the phone call.

Start by setting a standard that the phone must be answered by the third ring. People do not like to be kept waiting; answering the phone on the third ring is fairly prompt. The third ring on your end of the line might actually be the fourth ring on the other end. So, you are still getting to the phone in a relatively short period of time and you have set a performance standard by which everyone in your company can be measured. When you do your customer satisfaction surveys, ask customers how often the phone was answered by the third ring.

After you establish the three-ring standard, create a simple phone greeting that everyone uses. When you standardize the phone greeting, callers will come to expect your high level of professionalism, courtesy and customer service every time they call. They might even consider doing more business with you, simply because of the way you answer the phone. Your telephone answering script for all employees should be something like this: "Hello (or good morning, good afternoon, etc.), ABC Company. This is (*your name*). How may I help you?"

By asking how you may help them, you invite the caller into a friendly conversation. If you ask "May I help you?", you invite them to say no. When you ask "*how?*" you open the door for them to give you more information. And, the only way you can determine what a customer needs and how you can best sell them something to satisfy those needs is to ask questions.

Let's summarize the beginning of great telephone customer service: answer the phone within three rings and greet the caller, identify your company, identify yourself, and ask how you may help. The caller then begins a dialogue with you.

The concept of telephone dialogue is critical to your success. Dialogue means a two-way conversation; between you and the caller. A monologue is a one-way conversation; too often, businesses get involved with monologues while they tell the customer everything they think the customer wants to hear or know. If the business person kept quiet for just a few minutes and let the customer talk, he or she would learn a great deal about why the customer called in the first place.

During a telephone dialogue, keep in mind that the customer cannot see you, so, you need to use other techniques to establish rapport with that customer.

► Watch your tone of voice. Speak in a pleasant manner so that your tone conveys the message of your words. You will have a hard time communicating if the caller picks up any incongruity. If you do not believe this, think about a time when you have been in a conversation or argument with someone close to you. They say something and you become upset. They ask you why you are upset, because they do not perceive they said anything that would hurt your feelings. You say that it is not *what* they said but *how* they said it.

This is the key. How you say something conveys more meaning than what you say. In fact, communications research shows us that how you say something accounts for 93 percent of the meaning of your message, while only 7 percent is accounted for by what you say. So, when you speak with someone over the phone, keep your tone upbeat and positive. Do not let it convey annoyance, boredom, impatience or a lack of interest in what the customer is saying. If you do, they might just hang up and never call back.

You can make sure you always use a positive tone of voice by putting a smile on your face when you pick up the phone. Your smile will be broadcast over the phone lines to the caller. Both of you will be more relaxed and the conversation will take on a more personal and friendly tone.

► Use words and sentences the caller can understand. It does you no good to show off how smart you are by using technical terms, industry jargon, acronyms, or "big" words. Speak so the caller understands you. Do not mumble. Enunciate your words, especially if there are regional accent differences. Speak slowly, but not so slowly you become boring. Even if you and this caller have different accents, speak in your normal volume; there is no reason to speak louder just because you are from one part of the country and the caller is from another.

► Listen to everything the customer has to say. Listening becomes even more important during telephone customer service, because you cannot see the caller's reactions and responses to your words. So, listen for the actual words and the hidden meanings between the words.

If you just pay attention to these few suggestions, your telephone customer service skills will increase dramatically. You already know how important it is to answer the phone promptly, greet the caller correctly, and speak in an ordinary conversation voice. It is just as important to do the following to make a good impression on your caller.

Seven More Great Telephone Customer Service Tips

1. Always have a pad and pencil or pen near the phone. It is very annoying to a customer who calls to give you some information if you tell him or her to wait while you find a pen and paper. If pen and paper are near the phone at all times, you can begin taking notes as soon as you answer the call.

2. If you are computerized, access the customer's record as soon as they identify themselves on the call. This way, you have all the information you need about the customer—who they are, past purchase history, series of complaints, requests and needs, etc.—right there in front of you. You can even type notes to update the record on the spot.

   A customer database does wonders for your business. When customers from long ago call me up to discuss something, they ask if I remember what we talked about last year, or two years ago; they are amazed at how accurate my memory is. In reality, I read them the notes in my customer database. Regardless of the type of business you are in, a customer database can be crucial to your success as an operator and a customer service provider.

3. When you answer a customer's call, "own" the call. If the customer requests information or asks you to resolve a problem, try to take care of it. Customers appreciate being able to call a business and only speak with one person. Customers often resent being transferred, especially when they believe the call could have been handled by the person who answered it.

4. When you must transfer a customer, bridge the call with the customer and with the person who will receive the call from you.

   If you have to transfer a customer to another member of the staff, ask the customer if they mind being put on hold while you transfer the call to someone else who can help them more effectively. After they give you "permission," put them on hold, transfer the call, and tell the person who will receive the call exactly what the customer told you. Almost nothing is more irritating for a customer than to be transferred around in a company, and asked to repeat his or her story again and again. The customer should be able to tell the story once and you should be able to communicate that situation to the staff member who will handle the situation.

   Extend the same courtesy to the customer if you have to put them on hold for any other reason—ask for and get permission before you put them on hold. And, if you put them on hold, make sure you come back to the phone every thirty to sixty seconds to tell them how much longer you expect to be. Customers on hold perceptually double or triple the actual waiting time, which results in an annoyed or irate customer.

   One very efficient option is a computer program, hooked into your phone line, which transfers the customer's record and your current update as you transfer the call. This allows the staff member who finally takes care of the customer to have access to everything immediately, without asking the customer to repeat the story. While this type of software and communication systems networking is very expensive and not for every business, it makes a great impression on the customer.

5. When you complete the conversation, thank the customer for calling and gently hang up the receiver—do not slam it down. And do not start talking to someone else before you hang up the receiver. Obviously, this is especially important if you are using a speaker phone. Sometimes, staff members make a comment about a

customer to another staff member when they believe the phone is on the hook or the speaker is off. Unfortunately, this is not always the case and the customer hears the remark. Before you or anyone else says anything about a call they just completed, make sure the receiver is on the hook and the speaker is off.

6. If you call a customer who puts you on hold, wait on the line—do not put them on hold until they come back to you. It sends a poor message and provides a bad impression if you put them on hold without asking their permission while you attend to something else.

7. Whether they call you or you call them, always be enthusiastic, friendly, and positive. Your attitude and mood will be contagious and the customer will enjoy doing business with such a positive person. If this is a customer's first contact with your company, you will make an especially positive first impression. Customers will carry that impression with them for a long time.

How to Say What You Say Even Better

Based on the words and the tone you use during a telephone call, innocent comments, questions and remarks can come off very negative to customers. Picture in your mind and listen in your head to the different variations of the ways the following words can be said. More often than not, the tone of the voice messes up the entire mood of the conversation. As you read the following situations, think about how you feel if you are on the receiving end of the remark and how your customers feel when your staff talks in this manner.

1. You call a business and, when you ask to speak to a specific person, the receptionist says "Who's calling?" That is it—nothing else. Just "Who's calling?" How does it make you feel? Do you feel uncomfortable? Out of sync? Strange? Think about how your customers feel if this is done to them. To soften the "inquisition atmosphere," the receptionist might ask "May I ask who's calling, please?" or "May I have your name, please?"

Similarly, when the person who answers asks "What is this in regards to?", the caller often feels like they are on the witness stand. Train your people to ask "What is this in reference to, please?", or "May I please tell _____ what this is in reference to?"

2. You ask to speak to someone who tells you the person you are calling is not there. Then, the person who answers the phone volunteers that he or she does not know where the individual is or when he or she will be back. Some people will go so far as to tell you the person you want to speak with is in the bathroom. All they really need to say is "He/she is not in the office (or is in a meeting). I expect him/her back at _____ ."

3. You have to leave your name and number for a return phone call. Instead of politely asking you "May I have the correct spelling of your name and your phone number, please?", the person who answers your call asks "What's your name and number?"

4. You call a business and ask for information. The person you speak with says "Lemme get that for you." There are a number of better ways to say this. "Please hold while I get (obtain) that information for you." "Would you mind holding while I get that for you?" and "Please be patient while I get that information for you," all make much better impressions on the caller.

5. Avoid words like "yeah,""uh-huh," "nope," "un-un (for no)." Use "yes," "no," "I see," "I understand," "I hear you," in place of slang phrases or grunts.

Remember that you and your staff are professionals and represent your business in a professional manner. What your staff says on the phone and how they say it definitely affects customers' perceptions of your business. Many times I have chosen not to do business with a company simply because of the way I have been treated on the phone. And, many other times I have decided to buy from a company just because of the way they handled my telephone call.

The ultimate compliment related to telephone customer service is when a customer calls you personally to tell you how wonderfully they were treated on the phone by one of your employees. Keep this list of Telephone Reminders in mind to provide great telephone customer service and you may find yourself inundated with calls about how great your people are on the phone:

Telephone Reminders

1. Greet the caller pleasantly and promptly.

2. Identify yourself and your department to the caller.

3. Use the caller's name.

4. Every call is an important one.

5. Be tactful when refusing a request due to company policy or another reason. Stress what you can do, not what you cannot do.

6. Take the time to be helpful. If you cannot help the caller, and only if you cannot personally help them, connect them with someone who can help.

7. Say, "please," "thank you," and "you're welcome."

8. Keep your promises; return calls promptly.

9. Treat all callers as customers. Treat all customers as friends.

10. When leaving messages, always leave your first and last name and your telephone extension.

11. Do not leave a caller on hold for more than sixty seconds without coming back on the line.

12. Always ask, "Is there anything else I can do for you?" before you say goodbye.

Skill 5: Handling Angry Customers

Every business has its share of upset or angry customers. Some businesses deal with them well—others, not so well. The surprising fact is that it is really very easy to handle most angry customers. You just have to know how to do it—know what they need from you right at that moment, and what they expect of you after that.

Let's look at some real-world examples of how to totally blow a situation and then some examples of how to effectively deal with an angry customer.

► A supermarket shopper was very upset about what she thought was an overcharge on her order. She was sure she had been overcharged on several items even though the bar codes on the items were read by light beams and the price was rung up automatically in the cash register. She accused the cashier of cheating her. The cashier became flustered and kept telling the shopper that the machine reads the codes and rings up the cost automatically; she had nothing to do with the prices. The shopper did not care. She kept yelling, more and more loudly, that she was being cheated. As the customer's volume level rose, the cashier started to cry. When the store manager finally came over to see what was going on, the shopper started yelling at the store manager about being cheated. The store manager yelled back, "If you don't like our prices, don't shop here! We don't need your business anyway!"

Your Turn   *Answer the following question:*

► What would you have done?

► A passenger on a cross country flight had reserved a special meal, which was not on the flight. At least that is what the passenger was told. He started to get upset and loud with the flight attendant, berating the airline for "always screwing up." The flight attendant told him that the airline was not to blame for the mix-up with his meal;

it was either his travel agent's fault or the catering company's fault. The passenger could eat another meal or "eat nothing at all."

Your Turn

Answer the following question:

► What would you have done?

A customer comes into a business and does not see what he or she wants, or comes in with a complaint. The employee he deals with cannot seem to work with this customer or provide him with what he wants. The customer gets irate and yells, becoming angrier by the minute. The staff member either walks away or yells back at the customer.

None of these examples is hard to believe. They happen all the time, even though everyone has heard that the customer is always right. The important question to answer is: how will you and your employees handle the angry customer?

More than anything else, an angry customer wants you to listen to him. Listening shows that you respect this person and are willing to treat him or her in a dignified manner. While this may sound psychological or philosophical, it is exactly what is happening in the customer's mind.

Here are some examples of how to handle an angry customer from my experience.

► A client asked me to arrange and promote his grand opening office party. We agreed in writing to a fee, plus all related expenses. When I presented him with the invoice, he got upset that he had to reimburse me $45 for expenses. He said that he was paying for my services and he should not have to pay for related expenses—even though he had signed the agreement. I listened to him and reminded him that he had agreed to reimburse me for my expenses. That got me nowhere; he continued to be upset. I asked him what I needed to do to make him feel better and to satisfy his concern over paying the expenses. He said that if I wiped the $45 off the invoice, he would be very happy. So I did.

By asking him what I could do for him then listening to his answer, and taking action on his answer, I calmed him down and kept a satisfied customer.

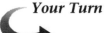

Your Turn   ***Answer the following questions:***

▶ Would you have done the same thing I did?

▶ Would you have done anything different or additional?

▶ My wife took our children to a well-known fast food restaurant for dinner, while I was on a business trip. When I returned the next day, she told me they had to wait twenty minutes to get their order, and three things were wrong with it. When the restaurant tried to correct it, something was still wrong with it. It took forty-five minutes for my family to complete their meal, and when they complained to the manager on duty, they received a very rude response.

I got upset when I heard this story, because we visit the restaurant quite often. I called the restaurant and spoke first with someone who was absolutely no help, so I said I wanted to meet with the manager. I was told when the manager would be in, and I said to tell her, "I'll be there." When I met later with the manager, she did everything perfectly to handle me as an irate customer. She listened to me, apologized for what happened, and then calmly asked me what would make me happy. I told her that my family expects prompt and courteous treatment, and that the meals should come out right the first time. She agreed, and asked that we give them another chance by coming in for dinner anytime we wanted, for free.

Your Turn   ***Answer the following question:***

▶ What would you have done?

These examples illustrate the good and the bad sides of dealing with angry customers. In a nutshell, listen carefully, calm the customer down, and find out what you must do to satisfy that customer. The rest of this chapter will help you get a better understanding of what angry customers are thinking and feeling, what they could be upset about—it may have nothing to do with you, your business or what they bought from you—what they want from you when they are upset, and a ten-step process to help you better manage your upset customers.

Why Customers May Be Upset

There are numerous reasons why customers may be upset. Some of them have to do with what they bought from you, while other reasons are more personal. You can find out what is bothering customers by noticing their appearance and physical posture when they approach you, and then asking appropriate questions.

Your Turn

Here is a comprehensive list of reasons customers might be upset. Take a look at your business and see which of these items apply.

▶ Are there any reasons you need to add to the list?

Customers Could be Upset Because They

▶ Are in a hurry.

▶ Had expectations that have not been met.

▶ Were already upset at someone or something else (boss, spouse, kids, a co-worker).

▶ Are tired, stressed or frustrated.

▶ Feel like a victim—not much power in their life in general.

▶ Feel no one will listen to them unless they yell and make a scene.

▶ Have to prove they are right.

▶ Walk around with a chip on their shoulder—nothing is right in their lives.

- ► Were promised something that was not delivered.

- ► Were treated indifferently, rudely or discourteously.

- ► Were told one thing by one staff member and something else by another.

- ► Acted on something told them by a staff member, and it was wrong.

- ► Feel you, or someone in your organization, has an unpleasant attitude toward them.

- ► Do not feel they were listened to.

- ► Have certain personal prejudices towards you—they may not like your clothes, gender, race, etc.

- ► Feel they can manipulate you to get what they want if they make a lot of noise.

- ► Are suspicious of your organization—think your organization or you are dishonest.

- ► Made a wrong assumption about what your organization would do for them.

- ► Were told they have no right to be angry.

- ► Were given a smart or flippant reply.

- ► Were transferred on the phone without consent.

- ► Were improperly screened on the telephone.

- ► Were embarrassed at doing something incorrectly.

- ► Had their integrity or honesty questioned.

- ► Had you or someone in your organization argue with them.

- ► Believe you do not have enough training to handle their situation properly.

- ► Are confused, overwhelmed, nervous, anxious or worried.

► Are defending their ego or self esteem.

► Feel ignored.

► Are in a bad mood and take it out on you.

► Have been treated poorly in similar circumstances in the past.

► Do not speak or understand the language.

► Waited an extended period of time.

► Believe they will not receive good service from you.

► Just are.

If you have employees, have you trained them to be aware of these possibilities and how to handle the situations that arise?

What Customers Want From You When They Are Angry

It is important to know what customers want from you when they are angry. You know that a customer who is upset and complains about something wants his or her complaint resolved. Customers who return items want an even exchange, a credit or a refund. These are the situational things they want from you.

On a personal level, customers who are angry and complaining want to be:

► Listened to

► Understood

► Empathized with

► Respected and have their dignity and integrity maintained

► Valued

► Made to feel important

► Made to feel right

► Made to feel intelligent

- ► Appreciated for their business

- ► Taken seriously

- ► Assured the problem will not happen again

- ► Guaranteed immediate action

- ► Relieved of their anger and anxiety

- ► Compensated in some way

Your Turn ***Answer the following questions:***

- ► From your own experiences, what else do angry and complaining customers want from you?

- ► When you have been an angry customer, how were you treated?

- ► How did that make you feel?

- ► What would you want that person to do differently?

- ► What would you have done differently if you were the service provider instead of the customer?

What To Do When A Customer Is Angry

Follow this ten-step process whenever you encounter an angry customer.

1. **Don't Argue:** Acknowledge the customer's right to be angry and upset.

2. **Listen Carefully:** Allow the customer to speak and completely ventilate his or her feelings. Although it may seem like an eternity, give him or her anywhere from thirty seconds to two minutes of uninterrupted talk time. You will find that most people cannot sustain a high level of emotional anger for this period of time if you just listen and do not interrupt. Use your active, reflective and empathic listening skills to encourage the customer to keep talking.

3. **Apologize and Use Reflective Communication Skills:** Tell the customer you are sorry and restate the problem as you understand it. Also let them know that you are going to do everything possible to help them out, because you do not want them to continue being upset.

4. **Show Empathy:** Let the customer know you understand the problem from his or her point of view and how he or she feels.

5. **Ask Questions:** Questions will help you clarify the problem and the customer's interpretation of it. Asking questions keeps you from making a statement that the customer may perceive as placing the blame elsewhere or passing along the responsibility to resolve the issue. Make certain you completely understand the situation.

6. **Thank the Customer:** That's right, say "thank you" to the customer for bringing the issue to your attention. If you remember, only a small portion of your customers actually complain. So treat every complaint or angry encounter as an improvement opportunity. Someone is helping you get better—thank them.

7. **Make Restitution:** Explain exactly what you will do to resolve the issue—only after you have calmed the customer down and he or she is speaking with you, rather than yelling or venting at you. After you explain what you will do, make sure the customer understands the process and accepts your efforts.

8. **Do What You Promise:** Deliver on your promise of restitution. This is another opportunity to cement a customer's loyalty. If you underpromise and overdeliver, the customer will love you for life. If you do not do what you promise, you will never have another chance.

9. **Follow-up:** Follow-up is essential to your continued success. Angry customers may feel better in the moment they leave you, but it is up to you to make certain their angry feelings do not return later. Call them or write them to make certain they still feel good about what you did for them.

10. **Give Them Something:** Give them something for their troubles. It can be a discount on their next purchase, something for free, or anything you can think of. The important thing is that the customer believes you have gone out of your way for them when they were angry and that you really want their business, because you are willing to give them a gift as a thank you for continuing to do business with you.

This entire process is based on effective communication. Here are a few service-related phrases you can use to help you even more.

"I agree with you that . . ."

"I appreciate that . . ." or "I appreciate your . . ."

"I respect that . . ." or "I respect you for . . ."

"I understand . . ."

"You're right."

Using these agreement or bridge phrases will improve all aspects of your communication. These phrases also work well when a disagreement occurs in any interpersonal situation.

Other Types of Difficult Customers

You are going to run into all types of customers in your business, not just angry ones. While you will probably remember the angry ones the most, and chances are they will give you the most trouble, consider these other types of customers: the impatient customer, the confused customer, the frightened customer, the insulted customer, the interrupting customer and the talkative customer. Each type can be best handled in the manner described on the following graphic. When you handle these customer types, your goal is to make sure the customer comes away feeling positive about you and your business.

Seven Types of Difficult Customers and How to Handle Them

THE ANGRY CUSTOMER

Listen.
Don't argue. Avoid letting emotion get to you.
Show respect.
Ask tactful questions.
Offer positive, constructive ideas.

THE IMPATIENT CUSTOMER

Respond quickly.
Get down to business; omit detail unless the customer requests it.
Reassure the customer the job will be done well, completely, and on time.
Make the customer feel important.

THE CONFUSED CUSTOMER

Find out what has caused the confusion.
Use sincerity to gain trust.
Keep explanations brief and to the point.
Reassure the customer about the proper decision.
Be patient and provide guidance.

THE FRIGHTENED CUSTOMER

Do whatever you can to alleviate the fear.
Speak calmly and softly.
Use sincerity to build trust.
Reassure the customer that everything will be okay.
Offer simple explanations.
Stay with the customer until his or her fear subsides.

THE INSULTED CUSTOMER

Apologize.
Be calm and brief.
Reassure with positive manner.
Allow the customer to talk it out. Listen.
Follow up with full explanations.

THE INTERRUPTING CUSTOMER

Ask not to be interrupted.
Be firm, be brief, and be polite.
Give explanations of key points.
Maintain conversational tone of voice.
Show restraint.

THE TALKATIVE CUSTOMER

Listen.
Be polite and firm.
Apologize and explain your time constraints.
Focus on giving the customer what he or she wants.
Tell the customer you will get back to him/her in _____ minutes.

Skill 6: Complaint Management

For years, many people in business believed that customer service was nothing more than handling complaints. Many businesses located their "Customer Service Department" (read complaint department) in a back room or remote corner, so that a complaining customer would not disturb other people. Only recently have businesses realized the importance of proactive customer service and that complaint management is an integral part of their success.

The concept of complaint management is technically called "service recovery and restitution." This is a fancy term for doing what it takes to resolve a customer's problem and make him or her happy. As you read earlier in the Startling Service Statistics, almost three-quarters of the people who complain to you will do business with you again if you resolve their complaint quickly and to their satisfaction. Many people and companies don't realize that their complaint management process can be both a proactive service tool and a sales tool. Later in this chapter you will learn tactics to do just that.

Let's discuss what I call "missed opportunities." The following stories are all true.

▶ At lunch with two friends, we ordered our meals—two hamburgers and a salad—at 12:30 pm. By 1:20, when the meals had not arrived, we called over the manager and told him we had not received our meals. He said he would look into it and disappeared off toward the kitchen. We never saw him again. Our meals arrived at 1:30, and we mentioned the one hour delay to the server. She told us there was nothing she could do about it, especially since it was not her fault or responsibility. As we left, we saw the manager and mentioned the poor service and attitudes to him. He commented, "If you don't like it, don't eat here again." You can be sure we never will go back.

Contrast this with a similar situation in another restaurant where the manager came out, apologized for the delay, offered to have the restaurant buy the meals, and gave us dessert coupons to come back another time. This second manager turned a complaint situation into an additional sales opportunity.

► Don bought a computer software program from a dealer. When he tried to install it on his machine, he could not get it to work. He called the software technical support line, as well as the store where he bought it. While all the people were helpful, the program still would not work. So, Don put the program back in the box and tried to return it to the store. Unfortunately, he did not have his receipt, and the person who sold him the program had the day off. The sales clerk said he could not help.

The company policy was not to accept returns without a receipt, regardless of the reason. Don only wanted to exchange the software or get a credit. He did not want any money back. But, the sales clerk followed the store policy to the letter. It did not matter to him that the store's label was on the box. All that mattered was that this customer was bothering him about some return without a receipt. And, the clerk was not going to go against company policy.

Do you think Don will ever buy software from that company again? Do you think he will tell all his friends and associates to stay away from that store? Think about how much software you or your friends purchase for home and business use, and how much money this store lost by not effectively managing this customer's minor complaint.

You may think it was Don's responsibility to hold on to the receipt—it may have been. But, how many times have you lost a receipt and tried to make a return? And, did the store do it for you with no questions asked? Or, did they make you feel like you were a criminal for not following their policies and rules? It seems to me that the software store ran its business for its own convenience rather than that of the customer.

> ▶ Do you run your business that way, or do you do whatever it takes to effectively manage complaints and turn them into sales?

Managing Customer Complaints

One of the most influential factors related to customer satisfaction and perception of service quality is how you handle customer complaints. Many customers judge a company by how well they respond to complaints, refund requests or exchanges. In a nutshell, accept all refund requests and exchanges graciously, make them quickly, and do not question the customers as to why they are requesting the refund or making the exchange. Unconditional service will take you much further than anything else in developing satisfied customers who remain loyal and refer other customers.

When a customer comes to you with a complaint, do not view it as a problem. View it as a golden opportunity. Your customers, who have taken their valuable time to contact you with complaints, are also going to provide you with free information about how you can improve your business. They will also be telling you exactly what to do to make certain you satisfy them now and in the future. Listen to their complaints. Question them for more information. Beg them if you have to. Just make sure you find out exactly what the customer wants and then give it to him or her.

A customer who complains feels annoyed, cheated or victimized. That customer feels that his or her situation is the most important in the world. Understand these feelings and treat your customers accordingly. Remember that thirteen percent of your dissatisfied customers will tell up to twenty friends that they are unhappy with the way you do business. If you resolve their problems, 50 to 74 percent of these same customers will do business with you again. Adapt the following recovery program to your business and specific situation, and then train your employees to be sure it is implemented.

Service Recovery and Restitution Program

1. **Apologize.**

   First and foremost, say you are sorry for the inconvenience the customer has experienced. Be sincere—the customer will notice if you are not. A sincere apology usually defuses the customer's anger. Also, you must personally accept responsibility for the problem occurring and its resolution. You do this even if you were not the original cause of the problem or complaint.

2. **Use restatement to clarify.**

   Restate the problem in your own words as the customer described it to you, to make certain you understand exactly what the customer means. Then, tell (and show, if possible) the customer that you will do everything possible to solve the problem and resolve the complaint immediately. Even if you cannot resolve the problem to their fullest satisfaction, the customer will perceive that you were sincere and definitely intended to help. The dissatisfaction will diminish.

3. **Show empathy.**

   Make certain you communicate clearly to your customers so that they understand that you know how they feel. Do not patronize or try to pacify them. Just show them and tell them you understand how they feel. Use phrases such as "I understand . . . ," "I know how you feel . . . ," and "I can see why you're upset." Also, emphasize that you are glad they brought the problem to your attention, because it gives you an opportunity to correct the situation.

4. **Give restitution.**

   Do whatever it takes at this point to satisfy the customer. Give the customer whatever he or she needs or wants or expects from you to resolve the complaint without giving away the store. After you resolve the complaint, go the extra mile and give the customer something else: a discount coupon, a free gift, or allow him or her to purchase another item at a sale price. Do something extra to add value to what might have been a bad situation.

5. Follow Up.

Check with all customers before they leave to make sure they are satisfied. Ask, "Have we resolved your complaint to your satisfaction?" Then, call them and write them a note within a week of the complaint resolution to make certain they are still satisfied. You may even want to include a sales coupon with your note. Make sure you continue to keep in touch with the customer. Going the extra mile will help you create and keep a loyal customer. Also, keep track of what you did and said as well as how the customer responded. This will help you the next time the customer does business with you.

Turning Complaints into Sales

There is no better time to try to upsell or make a new sale to customers than when you have resolved a complaint to their satisfaction. If you have listened carefully, focused on one complaint at a time and resolved it, and made a value-added offer to the customer just to show your appreciation for giving you the opportunity to resolve the complaint, you are ready to make another sale.

Think about it. Your customer is now extremely satisfied with what you have done. He or she is in a great mood and very happy to do business with you. All you have to do is build on this momentum to create an additional sale.

Use this basic five-step approach to manage complaints through service recovery and restitution. You may want to break the restitution step (#4) down into resolution (the action taken to resolve the complaint) and restitution (what you will do for the customer to compensate them for their inconvenience). This will help you manage customer complaints much more effectively.

Remember, customers whose complaints get resolved quickly and to their satisfaction are the most motivated buyers you will ever run into. They may not buy from you immediately, on the spot, but the odds are in your favor that they will eventually buy from you. So, be proactive in handling all your customer complaints, go through the recovery and restitution process, and turn the complaints into sales.

The basic approach for handling a complaint and keeping a customer is also a unique sales opportunity. A customer is more motivated to buy from you at the time you take special care of them—resolve their complaint—than at any other time. Once you resolve the complaint to their satisfaction, you can begin working on a new sale. Use these ten suggestions on turning customer complaints into additional sales to create loyal and long-term customers for your business.

1. Understand why the customer is complaining. Most probably, a need has not been satisfied or an expectation has not been met.

2. Listen attentively. The customer wants your undivided attention and respect concerning this problem, and he or she deserves to get it.

3. Handle one complaint at a time, even if the customer has several. You can manage a single complaint most effectively and have a better chance of turning that complaint into a sale than trying to handle two or three complaints at once.

4. Ask the customer what the needs were at the time of purchase and why those needs are not now being met. Find out how the current needs differ from the original, and why the change occurred.

5. Tell the customer that you understand the complaint and that you are sorry there is a problem. Assure the customer that you will do everything possible to resolve the complaint immediately.

6. Once you have resolved the complaint, discuss new sales offers and their benefits.

7. Handle any objections you may receive to the new sales offer, and continue to manage the original complaint if it comes up again.

8. Attempt to close the new sale resulting from the customer complaint as if it were an original sale. Sometimes, these "complaint sales" are easier because the customer has already made a purchase and knows how your product or service can satisfy a need.

9. If you cannot resolve the complaint to the customer's satisfaction, offer alternatives such as speaking to a person of higher authority, exchanging the merchandise, or refunding their money.

10. Up to 75 percent of the people who complain and have that complaint resolved immediately will make another purchase. Use this statistic to your advantage as you continue to try to close the "complaining" customer.

Resolving Complaints by Showing You C.A.R.E.

Here is another idea to support your complaint management efforts. When you resolve a service or performance problem, show the customer you care. If you care, your customers will reward you with their loyalty. To care properly for your customers, you must be:

Credible. Credibility, or your reputation, is really all you have in the business world. Customers must believe in your product or service, your customer service policies and procedures, your performance efforts and those of your staff. If they do not believe in you, they will not buy from you. Customers buy only for four reasons: to save or make money, to save time, to feel secure (have peace of mind) or to boost their egos. If you promise that your product or service will do one or more of these four things for your customers, then it better perform. It if does not, you must implement your service recovery program to ensure their satisfaction and loyalty.

Accessible. Customers want to be able to access your customer service system quickly and easily. They are already upset about something. Do not make it more difficult for them by passing them from employee to employee. Be accessible, approachable and customer friendly.

Reliable. Customers want to know what they can expect from your business. You must do what you say you will do at the time you say you will do it. You must get it right the first time, get it done for the customer on time, and then check with the customer to ensure satisfaction. Reliability comes from the consistency in the performance of your product or service and the consistency with which you treat customers. When you are reliable, customers know what to expect from you and they feel comfortable doing business with you.

Excellence. Do not accept anything less. You and your employees must strive for excellence all the time. Customers believe that they themselves are important and excellent, and they want to do business with excellent companies and people. Provide excellent customer service and you will have excellent customer retention. Provide excellent training programs for your staff and you will have excellent performers who will ensure retention of your customers. If your work is not excellent, it is not good enough. Your customers want excellence and so should you.

Retaining your customers must become part of your regular business life. Follow the five basic steps for recovery and restitution, manage complaints so that you can turn them into additional sales, and care for your customers. If you do so, you will keep your customers for a long time.

WHAT IS CUSTOMER SATISFACTION?

The most important factor in business today is customer service that leads to customer satisfaction. If your customer is not satisfied, he or she will stop doing business with you. All the things you do to provide excellent service are not important if you do not satisfy the customer.

Just what is customer satisfaction? It is the customer's perception that his or her expectations have been met or surpassed. He or she buys something and expects it to work properly. If it does, the customer is satisfied; if it does not, the customer is dissatisfied. Then it is up to the seller to find a way to fix the problem so that the customer can be satisfied. When the fix occurs to the customer's approval, he or she is satisfied. When it does not, the customer will "vote with his or her feet" and take his or her business elsewhere.

Satisfied Customers Buy More (and More Often)

It is a simple truth. Satisfied customers do more business with you more often. They purchase more each time around, and they purchase more often. They also refer their family and friends to you. The link between sales, service, satisfaction and profits is direct. The better you service a customer, the more a customer is satisfied, and the more he or she spends. The more customers spend, the more you sell. And, usually, when you sell more, your profits are greater.

Quality and service are the means to the ends of satisfaction and retention. Your main goal should be to produce a satisfied and loyal customer who will stay with you over time. Therefore, providing high quality and superior customer service are givens when you consider your ultimate goals of customer satisfaction and business success.

What Gets Measured Gets Done

This is a very true axiom. Whenever you measure something, it gets performed, completed and, usually, improved upon. That is why measurement techniques are so important to customer service success. Measurement is the critical component in determining if a company's service programs and overall performance are meeting or exceeding customer needs. It is why so many companies have begun measuring the satisfaction levels of their customers.

When you have a quantifiable number or measure to put on a behavior, people can see exactly what effect that behavior is having on their own and the company's performance. Asking customers to rate you on your levels of quality and service, and their level of satisfaction, virtually guarantees that you will work to improve your efforts in these areas.

Defining Customer Satisfaction

The definition of customer satisfaction is very simple. A customer is satisfied whenever his or her needs, real or perceived, are met or exceeded. So, how do you know what the customer needs, wants and expects? By now, you know—you ask! Then you provide what the customer wants and more. If this seems repetitious, you would be surprised to know how many companies just do not get it. Another definition of customer satisfaction is simply whatever the customer says it is.

These definitions may seem very simplistic. They are simple and elegant by design. Using these definitions will enable you to accurately measure customer satisfaction levels in your company or organization. Your measurement objectives are simply to find out what your customer thinks and how he or she defines satisfaction. Then, you can build your measurement techniques around your customers' objectives and definitions.

The Benefits of Measuring Customer Satisfaction

The primary benefit of a measurement program is that it provides people with immediate, meaningful and objective feedback. They can see how they are doing right now, compare it to some standard of excellence or performance, and decide what they must do to improve on that measurement.

Have you ever asked yourself why basketball is so popular? It is because the player knows immediately if he or she succeeded. Performance is measured by the ball going through the basket or not, and the player is motivated to try again. This occurs whether or not the shot was successful.

Measurement provides people with a sense of accomplishment, a feeling of achievement. Measurements can also form the basis for a reward system that can only be successful if it is based on objective and quantifiable data.

How will you know which employees or work teams to reward for improving service and increasing customer satisfaction if you do not measure their performance?

The benefits of measuring customer service and customer satisfaction can be summed up in these five items:

1. Measurement provides people with a sense of achievement and accomplishment, which translates into superior service to customers.

2. Measurement provides people with a baseline standard of performance and a possible standard of excellence that they try to achieve, which will lead to improved service and increased customer satisfaction.

3. Measurement offers the performer immediate feedback, especially when the customer is measuring the performer or your company.

4. Measurement tells you what you must do to improve customer service and customer satisfaction and how you must do it. This information can also come directly from the customer.

5. Measurement motivates people to perform and achieve higher levels of productivity.

Why We Measure Customer Satisfaction

Before you can measure something, you must know what you are measuring and why. The following material will introduce you to the reasons for measuring customer satisfaction. When you know why you are doing this, and then you do it, implementing the results of your measurement program will proceed smoothly.

Your customer satisfaction measurement program must answer the who, what, when, where, how and why questions that are essential for success.

▶ **Who** will measure customer satisfaction? The answer is everyone.

▶ **What** must be measured? Everything and anything that affects the customer.

▶ **When** must you measure? Often.

▶ **Where** do you measure? Throughout the entire company and every process that has an effect on customer satisfaction.

▶ **How** do you measure? You establish performance standards and criteria that are quantifiable and that you can evaluate your performance against by using hard numbers and data.

▶ **Why** do you measure? To learn how to improve and increase customer satisfaction.

Let's discuss the seven basic reasons for conducting these measurements.

Reason #1: To Learn About Customer Perceptions

Customers are individuals, and each person will perceive things differently in the same situation. While many measurement programs attempt to get at mass averages from which to build or rebuild customer service programs, it is imperative that you at least consider identifying each customer's individual perceptions.

The perceptions you are trying to identify include: what customers look for in a business such as yours; why customers do business in your industry; what has caused them to change suppliers or providers in the past; what might make them change again in the future and how soon; what are their criteria for acceptable service quality performance; what must they receive to be minimally satisfied; what must you do to make them extremely satisfied; and what you must do for them so they will continue to do business with you.

Your Turn   *On this chart, fill in what you know about your customers with respect to these perceptions. Feel free to add to and modify the list as you see fit.*

Perceptions To Identify	Your Knowledge
What Customers Look For	
Why Customers Do Business in the Industry	
Reasons for Most Recent Change of Suppliers	
Possible Reasons for Future Change	
Criteria for Acceptable Service Quality	
Criteria for Minimally Satisfied	
Criteria for Exceptionally Satisfied	
Criteria for Retention and Repurchase	

Reason #2: To Determine Customer Needs, Wants, Requirements and Expectations

Your customer satisfaction measurements must determine how customers feel about the product or service they purchased and the service they received. It must also identify what customers need and want from you. You must find out what they require of you in the way of product/manufacturing specifications or program content, as well as what they expect you to provide during the overall sale and service encounter.

It is vitally important to the success of your measurement program that you learn about customers' current and future needs. Too many companies ask customers about a recent purchase, without ever trying to find out why they purchased it, what personal and psychological need the purchase satisfied, how they plan to use the purchase, what they expect from the purchase, and what they expect their needs to be in the future.

For example, let's say you build mousetraps, and you have just built the best mousetrap the world has ever seen. Now someone once said that if you build a better mousetrap, the world (read customers) will beat a path to your door. That is assuming they need, want and require a better mousetrap. If your customers have no need for mousetraps, now or in the future, they will not buy them from you. You would have the world's greatest mousetrap and no customers.

When you measure customer satisfaction, measure what they need, want, require and expect from you—and why.

Reason #3: To Close the Gaps

This reason for measuring customer service and customer satisfaction is so important, it is elaborated here even though it has already been discussed. Many gaps exist between customers and providers. Measuring these gaps is the only way to close them. All the gaps are based on differences in perception between what the business believes it provides and what the customer perceives he or she receives. These are the more important gaps that have been identified through research:

► **The gap between what a business thinks a customer wants and what the customer actually wants**

This is like having a company build that better mousetrap and inform the public it needs to buy it, when all the customers want is a piece of cheese. You and your business can never know what a customer truly wants unless you directly ask the customer. Use your measurement tools to inform the customers of what you think they may want; then allow them to tell you specifically what they want. The difference in perceptions is the gap you must close here.

► **The gap between what a business thinks a customer has bought and what a customer perceives has been bought**

It really does not matter what the business sold if the customer perceives he or she did not receive exactly what the customer was supposed to purchase. A mule instead of a horse, a regular stereo instead of a surround-sound stereo, or a training program that promises one set of results, yet the customer believes those results were not achieved—all create this type of gap.

The gap exists because the customer does not perceive the purchase in the same way that the business perceives the sale/purchase. Even if the business is right, the customer will feel cheated and dissatisfied. It is up to the business to close the gap and make certain the customer is satisfied.

► **The gap between the service quality the business believes it is providing and what the customer perceives is being provided**

This is very similar to the preceding problem, in that the business believes one thing and the customer believes another. This gap usually occurs either when the business has a certain way of servicing its customers that differs from how the customers would provide the service, or when the business has customer service policies that it tends not to change for each individual customer, and neglects to inform the customer of the policies. Both parties make decisions without benefit of all the available information. The customer does not know the business has certain policies and feels slighted by the apparent lack of service. The business may never know that the customer feels slighted.

► The gap between customers' expectations of service quality and actual performance

The problems that exist if this gap occurs are quite obvious. If you do not know what your customers expect of you, and you give them something completely different, or even slightly different, you can be sure they will not be satisfied. You must do everything possible to learn what your customers expect of you, and then deliver it to their satisfaction.

► The gap between service promises and actual delivery

Many times a company promises to deliver a certain level of service quality and is unable to meet that promise. Making the promise raises the level of expectation of the customer, and not delivering on it creates an unhappy customer. The simplest way to close this gap is to underpromise and overdeliver.

Your Turn

Closing these gaps is critical to your success in satisfying and retaining customers. Answer the following questions, which will help you close the gaps and, hopefully, make sure they never occur.

► Have you asked your customers what they need, want and expect from you?

► Is your company committed to providing superior service quality based on your customer research?

► Do you have a clear idea of how your customers make purchase decisions?

► Do you know what criteria your customers use to determine if they are satisfied?

► Have you overpromised on your delivery capabilities?

- ▶ Do your customers perceive you can meet their needs and expectations?

- ▶ Do you understand your customers' needs and expectations?

- ▶ Do you have a performance-measurement system in place to help identify customer needs, wants, and expectations and how well you meet those requirements?

- ▶ Do you have a recovery program in place to turn a dissatisfied customer around or to recapture a lost customer?

- ▶ Do your standards of service quality performance and customer satisfaction match the perceptual standards developed by your customers?

You can probably add several more questions to this list from your own experiences. These ten will serve as an introductory guide for you as you attempt to close the service satisfaction gaps that may exist for your business.

Reason #4: To Inspect What You Expect In Order to Improve Service Quality and Customer Satisfaction

You must set standards of performance, inform your staff and your customers of those standards and then measure your actual performance against those standards. When you set goals for your business based on your customers' requirements and expectations and publicly measure your performance toward those goals, you have an excellent chance of improving your levels of service and customer satisfaction.

The improvement comes from knowing where you are compared to where you want to be or where you should be, and taking the steps, based on the measurements, to improve your performance. Since your standards were developed in conjunction with customer perceptions, your ability to meet or exceed those standards—or fall short—will give you a good indicator of how satisfied your customers will be and what you must do in the future.

Reason #5: Because Improved Performance Leads to Increased Profits

While there is no guarantee that this will occur, it is a safe assumption that if you improve your service performance and delivery, you will probably benefit from increased profits. More people will want to buy from you, thereby increasing the volume contribution to profits. Also, as your level of service quality goes up along with levels of customer satisfaction, you can conceivably charge more money for your goods and services. This increased price, combined with the decreased costs you get from quality processes, will also lead to greater profitability.

Reason #6: To Learn How You Are Doing and Where You Go From Here

There are many very good reasons to measure your service quality performance and customer satisfaction levels. This one may be the most important of all. While you must know what gaps may exist and how to close them, what your customers need and expect and how they perceive the world, you need to know how you are doing right here, right now. Plus, you must be able to gather information on what you should be doing in the future.

Customer research provides you with this information. Customers will tell you if you are satisfying them now and what you must do to satisfy them in the future. They will tell you if you need to change your business strategy and/ or business direction. Measuring customers' perceptions of service quality and satisfaction levels is essential to your business success.

Reason #7: To Apply the Process of Continuous Improvement

This theme keeps coming up. If you do not continuously try to improve your service offerings, someone else will, and your customers will be their customers. Measure everything you do in relation to your own production of goods and services, and your delivery of them to your customers. Ask your buying customers as well as your employees how you can be better at what you do. Take their answers, suggestions and recommendations, and implement them within your business. Ask again and again. And keep making those incremental improvements.

Remember that your goal is to establish long-term relationships with satisfied customers. You do this by understanding and identifying your customers' needs, meeting and exceeding their expectations, closing or removing any perceptual gaps that may exist between what the business believes was delivered and the customers believe was received, and trying continuously to improve your service quality efforts.

A Final Thought on Measuring Customer Satisfaction

The concepts of continuous incremental improvement, superior customer service, and high quality are all related to customer satisfaction. However, if you have the chance to make a quantum leap in any of these areas to increase customer satisfaction, *do it*. Do not get locked into the mindset that you must do things a little bit at a time. If an opportunity for a major breakthrough in service quality or customer satisfaction presents itself, go for it. Teach your employees, associates and partners to go for it. You do not want to get locked into another "process" that is governed by policies and procedures that say you must make small, incremental improvements in order to be effective and successful. When the big jump presents itself, jump.

ASK YOURSELF

► How do you care for the customer?

► What prevents customer service from working in your business?

► Explain how you can use the telephone to more effectively provide excellent customer service.

► Identify the reasons customers may be upset with your business, and what you can do to change these situations.

► What policies and procedures do you have in place for handling complaints and turning them into sales?

► Describe the procedures you will implement to enhance your service recovery process.

CHAPTER
FIVE

CUSTOMER SERVICE AS A POWERFUL MARKETING TOOL

CUSTOMER SERVICE IS DONE FOR THE CUSTOMER

Only in the past several years have entrepreneurs and business owners realized that customer service is not something that is done *to* a customer, but rather something that is done *for* a customer. Throughout the early part of the 1980s, businesses perceived customer service more as a reactive, complaint-handling activity to deal with customer concerns and problems. Not until the end of the decade, when a great deal of customer research was publicized, did companies begin to understand the importance of customer service in the marketing mix.

Companies learned that if they were proactive with their customer service efforts, they could acquire and keep customers more easily. Customers were drawn to companies that clearly communicated their business message: The products and services had value and they were supported by the company. An even more proactive approach was the offering of guarantees.

While guarantees (and warranties) often came with manufactured products when they were purchased, many companies never explicitly communicated their guarantees to the public. As customers became more educated and aware of what they received for their dollars, they began demanding companies support what they sell. Those companies that promoted—marketed—their guarantees also acquired customers more easily and at a lower cost. That is because the risk of the purchase is transferred from the customer to the seller.

The following true story demonstrates how customer service and guarantees can be used as a marketing tool to get and keep a customer for life.

I do a great deal of writing and publishing as part of my consulting practice. Sometimes, the only place I can get current information is from books that I purchase from bookstores. I spend several thousand dollars a year on book purchases. Every bookstore claims they will allow you to return a book or exchange it if you are not satisfied with it.

I approached the manager of Bookstore A, a large chain store that had some of my books on the shelves, and told him about my work. I explained that, from time to time, I need to purchase books for research, and if they do not pan out, I would like to return them for a refund or exchange. He agreed to this because it was a posted store policy. However, he did not communicate our "agreement" to all his employees. After several months when I made many purchases and only a few returns, an employee told me that I would not be allowed to exchange books—all my purchases were final. When I searched out the manager, I learned that he was on vacation and no one else could do anything about the situation, since they did not know of our arrangement.

I went to Bookstore B, spoke with the manager, and told her my situation. She quickly realized that if I purchased only $1,000 worth of books, instead of $2,000 to $3,000 during the year from her store, and I exchanged $300 worth, she was way ahead of the game. She also knew that I would come back every year and possibly refer my friends.

Which store do you think gets my business? Obviously, it is Bookstore B, which honors its guarantee and goes out of its way to make my situation more beneficial for me. This story shows you how customer service can be used as a powerful marketing tool.

TWELVE CUSTOMER SERVICE MARKETING TECHNIQUES TO BUILD YOUR BUSINESS

In the rest of this chapter, you will learn twelve of the best customer service marketing techniques you can use to build your business:

- ► Frequent Buyer Programs
- ► Frequent Referral Programs

- ► Thank You Cards

- ► Holiday and Birthday Cards

- ► Newsletters/Letters of News

- ► Confirmation Calls

- ► Reward and Recognition Programs

- ► Recall and Reactivation Programs

- ► Satisfaction Guaranteed (Risk Reversal)

- ► Treating Employees as Customers

- ► Customer Special Events

- ► Strategic Customer Alliances

Each technique is described below. If you wonder what customer service has to do with marketing, ask yourself how customers decide what makes you different than your competitors and why they should buy from you. Customer buying decisions are based on the information they receive from your marketing communications. You can use these twelve techniques to build your business—when you hit on the right combination of these techniques for your specific business, you can actually double your business in twelve months or less, without any other marketing efforts.

Frequent Buyer Programs

These programs are similar to the Frequent Flier programs promoted by airline companies. When you fly often enough and far enough under any airline's program, you receive mileage credits that can be exchanged for free tickets, ticket upgrades or free vacations. The more you fly, the more credits you receive.

You can set up a similar program in your business for your customers. A Frequent Buyer program shows your customers how much you appreciate their business. The more they buy from you, the more you give back to them. You reward your best customers for continuing to do business with you on a regular basis. How you reward them is not as important as the fact that you do reward them. You will see in the section on Frequent Referral programs that your rewards do not have to be expensive. They just have to have a perceived value in the customer's mind.

Make sure it is easy for all your customers to be part of this program. Keep track of their purchases in your database program so you can identify who gets what type of reward. Here is an example of how you can motivate customers to buy from you on a regular basis.

Consider a retail store that punches a card for you every time you buy something. After ten or twelve purchases, your punch card is complete and you receive something for free or at a significant discount.

Think about what is going on here. The retailer gives you the card to motivate you to come back several more times, so that you can "earn" the reward. You hold on to the card (a semi-permanent record and reminder) and become more motivated as you get closer to having all the holes punched. It is not the size or cost of the reward that becomes important. It is the fact that you would get something for free for your purchases. The retailer rewards you and recognizes you for your efforts. You will learn more about the power of reward and recognition programs shortly.

The card becomes the marketing motivator to keep you coming back into the business to buy. You keep coming back because you want the reward. The same happens with Frequent Flier programs. People change their schedules just to go on the preferred airline so they can pile up the mileage and get their "deserved" rewards.

 Your Turn   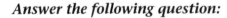 *Answer the following question:*

> ► What Frequent Buyer program is appropriate for your business?

Frequent Referral Programs

If your business depends on referrals, reward the people making referrals to you. Your rewards will reinforce their behavior, thereby creating a positive cycle and a mutually beneficial relationship.

The best way to use a Frequent Referral reward program is to develop it in tiers, or levels.

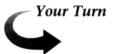

Your Turn

Here are some suggestions for rewards based on the number of referrals from one source. Fill in how you would reinforce referrals. Feel free to change the reward recommendation to suit your business or situation.

Number of Referrals	Reward Recommendation	My Reward
1	Thank you card	
2	Telephone call	
3	Flowers	
4	Small gift (under $10)	
5	Gift certificate (dinner for two)	

When the same person refers more than five people to you, do something special for that person. Then, start the Referral Reward program all over again. Remember, the size or the cost of the gift is not as important as giving the gift to show your appreciation.

If your customers do not mind having their names visible in your store or office, create a referral thank you bulletin board. Post the names of your current customers who refer new customers to you on this board each month. You can also post the number of referrals they have made. People usually like to see their name written on something, and this will give them the satisfaction of knowing you appreciate their efforts. Also, it may create a healthy competition among your customers to see who can refer more new people to you each month. They benefit because you reward and reinforce them, and you benefit from the new business and positive word of mouth.

Create a New Customer Welcome Bulletin Board. List the names of your new customers each month. This is the first step in a proactive customer retention program. When people see that you care enough to put their name up for everyone else to see, they will go out of their way to help you in your business and to remain loyal to you.

Thank You Cards

One of the most effective customer service marketing techniques is to write a thank you card and send it to someone who has bought something from you. It takes only a little extra effort on your part. Fortunately for you, few businesses use this powerful and inexpensive marketing technique.

If you do not want to write out a card for every customer that purchases, have cards preprinted with a message that shows your appreciation, or use your computer to personalize a form letter thank you note.

Do thank you cards work? Just ask yourself how good you feel when you receive one and how your positive thoughts of the person who sent it increase.

Your Turn   *Answer the following question:*

   ► What type of Thank You's will you send to your customers?

Holiday and Birthday Cards

People love to receive cards in the mail. It gives them an uplifting feeling to know someone is thinking of them at a special time. It is even more uplifting and surprising if the cards come from a business associate, rather than a family member or friend.

I strongly recommend you send holiday cards to all your customers. These can be Thanksgiving, Hanukkah, Christmas, New Year's or whenever cards. If you are worried about your cards getting lost in the holiday mail, send them out early—like around the 4th of July or Halloween. Sure, it is well before your customers might expect it, but, that is the point. It is so unexpected that they will remember you for it.

The same is true for birthday cards. If you can get the birth dates of your customers, they will be pleasantly surprised to receive birthday cards from you. This is a simple and inexpensive gesture on your part, which does take a little of your time. Yet, the payoff in additional purchases and referrals that you will receive from this customer is tremendous.

One word of caution: Never send anniversary cards. You cannot know if your customer has become separated or divorced since the last time you had contact with him or her. While this may seem like a minor point, I strongly suggest you stay away from these cards. I had a client who refused to listen to this advice. He sent an anniversary card to a couple who bought life insurance policies from him a few months earlier. It turned out, they bought the policies hoping that it would bring their marriage back together. Unfortunately, the agent did not know that, and he sent an anniversary card without confirming the situation. The couple separated two weeks before their anniversary, and each person in the dissolving marriage was so hurt by the card my client sent that they canceled the policies.

I highly recommend you do not take this type of chance. Finally, here is a way to extend the holiday card idea. You can give holiday gifts to your customers. These gifts don't have to be expensive. They just should have a perceived value in the minds of the customers.

Now, you may be thinking that you have hundreds or thousands of customers—or one day you will—and this could get expensive. You are right, it can become expensive. But, how much is that customer worth to you, and how much business does that customer bring to you each year? Is it worth $10 or $25 for a gift to show you appreciate his or her business?

Newsletters/Letters of News (LON)

Newsletters are a great way to keep customers informed of what is going on in your business. You can tell them information you need for them to know and, because it is coming from you free of charge, they will be only too glad to read it.

One way to keep customers involved with your business is to promote contests or other activities in the newsletter. Specify that they come to your store or office to win the contest. This is another good time to solidify their loyalty and make sure you retain them as customers.

A great variation of the newsletter is the Letter of News. Write a personal letter to each customer. Use a computerized customer database, which makes this task very easy and efficient. Mention all the items you would have mentioned in a newsletter. Your customers will be pleased that you took the time to write them a personal letter. An example of a letter of news is shown on page 129.

Your Turn

Answer the following question:

► What type of newsletter or letter of news is appropriate for your business?

Confirmation Calls

Telephone Confirmation Calls work well in any type of business. If you are in a service business where customers need to make appointments, you can call them a day in advance to remind them of the appointment. Your dentist or doctor probably does this. Or, if specific customers have

Sample Letter of News

Today's Date

Michael Mitchell
Any House
Anytown, USA

Dear Michael Mitchell:

I just wanted to thank you for continuing to do business with us. Our relationship is very important to me, and I'm sure it's been beneficial for you also. I wanted to take this opportunity to tell you about some of the great things that are happening in our business and how they can benefit you. As you know, we have provided both marketing consulting and training services for you in the past. Your comments indicated you were very satisfied and are interested in working with us again. Here is some exciting news to help you decide on when we can begin these programs.

New Marketing Book Gets Published

I have recently had the honor of having a marketing book published by Crisp Publications. It is called *Marketing Strategies for Small Businesses*. The book sells for $15.95. It is available to all our marketing consulting clients free of charge. If you participate in one of our marketing workshops, it is given to you as part of the workshop fee. It also reduces the cost of the workshop to you, since now there is no materials charge.

The Last Training Seminar You Will Ever Need

After more than 20 years of research in psychology, human behavior, human relations and communications, we have designed a sales training program that can help you achieve greater professional success, more sales, more friendships, deeper and more meaningful customer relationships and a better personal life. It is called *Extraordinary Selling Power,* and it teaches you about people's behavioral and interpersonal styles, communication styles and the basic principles of effective human relations. The program is customized to suit your needs and budget.

I hope this information has been helpful to you. Please feel free to call me at (813) 726-7619 if you have any questions. Or, just stop by to see us to say hello. We appreciate you as our customer, and we look forward to continuing our relationship with you.

Sincerely,

Richard F. Gerson, Ph.D.
President

P.S. My last customer service book, *Beyond Customer Service,* published by Crisp Publications, has just sold its 20,000th copy worldwide. Thanks for contributing to its success.

not been in to see you in some time, you can call them to see how they are doing and to inform them of a reason to come in now to do business with you. You will learn more about this in the Recall and Reactivation program section.

If your business is retail, you can personally call customers and invite them to a special sale. Department stores often do this by sending mailers to their credit card holders inviting them to a sale before inviting the general public. If this makes you feel special, think how much more special you will feel when someone calls you personally. (You will learn more about this in the Customer Special Events section.)

When you are unable to make all the calls personally, write out a basic script for someone else to call for you. You want your message of caring for the customer to come across loud and clear. Create a log sheet on which your caller can record the results of each call and can indicate whether or not the person will attend the appointment.

Your Turn   *Answer the following question:*

    ▶ When are confirmation calls appropriate for your business?

Reward and Recognition Programs

Recognizing and rewarding your customers should be a regular business practice. Sending thank you cards tells customers you recognize their importance to your business. Giving them gifts for referrals shows them how much you appreciate their efforts on your behalf. Offering them rewards for making repeat purchases informs them you understand their contribution to your business success. You can still do more to retain customers. First, recognize every customer who does business with you. Learn and use their names. If you cannot remember someone's name, at least acknowledge that you recognize that person as a regular customer. For new customers, go out of your way to learn their names and everything you can about them. They will appreciate your interest in them.

Next, make your customers feel important. Many businesses say they do this, but it is just not so. You have to give extra effort to make customers feel important, and once you do, you will keep them for life.

What are some ways you can make them feel important? Try these suggestions:

- ► Ask them about their family, especially their children or grandchildren.

- ► Congratulate them on some achievement or a job promotion.

- ► Ask for their advice on something related to your business.

- ► Tell them they look nice.

- ► Give them a surprise just for doing business with you.

- ► Give them a certificate that acknowledges them as a priority customer.

- ► Give them a plaque for being a great customer.

- ► Hold a Customer Appreciation Day (or Night) Sale.

You can probably think of several more ways to make people feel important. The key is to do this in a natural manner so that each customer feels and believes you are taking a special and sincere interest in him or her.

You can recognize and reward your customers in other ways. Give them special treatment. Hold a contest for your best customers and give the winner a trip as a grand prize. Give other winners gift certificates or dinners at fine restaurants. Print VIP cards for your best customers that entitle them to extra discounts.

All these ideas are strictly customer retention ideas—they have nothing to do with serving the customer during the time of a purchase. Yet, they are vitally important to the success of your business, because they create added value for the customer. They also create a sense of psychological loyalty. That makes it difficult for the customer to even consider switching to a competitor.

It is very easy for a competitor to price merchandise the same as you do, to give the same type of guarantees as you do, and to provide the same extensive and courteous service as you do. If that happens, the only thing that will make a customer choose to do business with you is the value-added service you provide.

Your Turn

This chart will help you create your own customer Reward and Recognition Program. Use the first column to describe the customer's action, the second to show how you will recognize the behavior, and the third to explain how you will reward the behavior.

Customer Action	How Recognized	How Rewarded
Samples:		
First Referral	Thank you note	Small discount
Second Referral	Telephone call	Box of candy
High Volume purchase	Telephone call/Letter	Dinner
_____	_____	_____
_____	_____	_____

Employee Recognition and Reward Programs

Any customer retention program must include recognition and rewards for your employees. Remember that employees are customers, too, and on some occasions, they are your most important customers. Show them you care about them as much as you do about external customers. Create a recognition and reward program for your employees, just as you do for your customers.

When you treat employees as customers, their morale will improve, and they will want to do well for the company. Furthermore, they will want to continue working for you.

Customers like to see the same faces all the time. Both your customers and your employees will enjoy the stability. People like doing business with people they know and like. Long-term employees provide that for you with your customers. Therefore, never forget or neglect your employees. Always treat them as customers. It is as important to retain them as it is to retain your external customers.

Your Turn

Answer the following question:

► What type of employee recognition and reward program is appropriate for your company?

Recall and Reactivation Programs

A Recall and Reactivation Program is such a powerful marketing tool that it can generate more revenue for your company than several of the other techniques combined. Reactivating your old customers can create new revenue streams you never thought possible. From a pure marketing perspective, this is one way to deploy "hidden" assets. We call them hidden because most business owners stop paying attention to them and forget they exist.

Here are several examples of ways you can recall and reactivate your old customers. If you need motivation to implement this type of program, remember that it costs five to six times more to get a new customer than it does to persuade an old customer to do business with you again.

► An automobile body shop sends its customers a coupon good for a free car wash and dent inspection six months after they complete a repair. Their goal is to get their customers back into the shop to see if there are additional services they can provide. To date, they service 20 percent of these returning customers.

► A dry cleaner keeps careful records of all its customers. When the computer flags customers who have not been in for ninety days, they send a letter to the customer inviting them to come back. Attached to the letter is a coupon for a free cleaning of a suit. This approach has reactivated 45 percent of the customers who have been sent the coupon. Plus, the dry cleaner surveys the returning customers to find out why they left in the first place, and uses the feedback to make improvements in operations and customer service.

► A consultant calls all his former clients (one-year old) to see how they are doing and to ask if there is anything he can do to help them. While no one responds immediately, he has received several calls for additional work a few months after his calls. These "Hello, How Are You?" calls to old customers are wonderful for re-establishing the rapport and trust that you once had, and for motivating them to do business with you.

When another consultant I worked with tried this approach, she generated over $20,000 in revenue in two months from former clients. This call approach is even more powerful if you do not ask for their business while you are on the phone.

Think of the sheer magnitude and potential of this technique. There are no acquisition costs, no time required to build trust and rapport, no energy investment to prove yourself, and no interference from competitors—just a simple phone call or letter asking your former customers how they are, what is happening in their personal and professional lives, offering them something for free just to come in to see you, sending them a small gift to show your appreciation for their past business, or simply doing something for them that they did not expect of you. All these actions on your part show former customers that you still care about them, that they are still important to you, and that you appreciate their business. If you keep in mind that *people do not care how much you know until they know how much you care,* and if you can constantly show people you care by providing great service, they will continue to do business with you.

Here is another twist on this customer service marketing approach. Many businesses send a thank you note or make an "obligatory" phone call after a customer makes a purchase. These efforts are often superficial at best. You can stand out from the crowd by literally calling everyone who buys from you and *sincerely* thanking them for their purchase.

After a purchase—especially an expensive one—customers often experience dissonance, feelings of uncertainty or uneasiness. They start to question themselves: Did I make the right choice? Did I really need to spend all that money? Should I have looked longer? Make a post-purchase reassurance phone call (recall the customer) and sincerely tell them that they made the right choice in both buying the item and buying it from you. Reassure them that you will always be available to provide them with the service you have promised and that they have come to expect from you. Then, follow this call up with a letter saying the same thing. Just doing this will separate you from the competition and create loyal customers who will stay with you "for life" and refer others to you.

Your Turn   *Answer the following question:*

► What type of recall and reactivation program is appropriate for your business?

Satisfaction Guaranteed (Risk Reversal)

Everyone in business today is offering some sort of guarantee. It has become the baseline standard for getting people to buy from you. You see these guarantees all the time:

Your satisfaction is guaranteed or your money back.

Full refund in 30 days with your receipt. Otherwise, a credit for exchange will be issued.

90-day, money back guarantee.

These are a few of the ways companies offer guarantees to satisfy customers, based on the psychological concept of risk reversal. Risk reversal means doing whatever it takes to remove the burden of purchasing from the customer.

People want extra value for every dollar they spend. They want to be assured they are getting exactly what they're paying for, and more. Guarantees are great, and you should offer them. But, since everyone offers a guarantee, you need to go a step or two further.

Provide a "Better Than Risk-Free Guarantee." Let people know that when they purchase something from you, they get what they buy, plus a small gift from you. If they decide they are not happy with the purchase and they return it, either for a refund or exchange, they still get to keep the gift.

This totally reverses the risk of purchasing. You take the "burden of proof" off the shoulders of the buyer and place it squarely on your own shoulders. You also plant a thought in the buyer's mind about how confident you are in your product or service. After all, would anyone—other than a highly confident provider—offer a gift with the purchase, knowing that the customer can return the purchase and still keep the gift?

Here is how the risk reversal concept works for one type of business.

Several of the major catalog houses allow you to return any purchase you make at any time for a full refund or exchange. They say if you are ever unhappy with your purchase or if it fails to perform to your expectations, you can return it at any time with no questions asked.

While this type of guarantee should make you feel very comfortable buying from these companies, you are probably wondering how you can apply this to your business. You may be concerned about people who will take advantage of your guarantee. Let me put your fears aside.

First, applying the risk reversal concept to your business is easy. Just offer your "better than your competitors" standard guarantee and then give them a small gift in addition to the purchase. Let the customers know they can bring back their purchase at any time and you will exchange it or refund their money. You can set standards for the return, if you want to.

Second, only a small number of people will take advantage of you. Let's say it is about 5 percent of all the customers you have. Are you going to run your business to stop the 5 percent from taking advantage of you, or are you going to service the 95 percent who are great customers and who will buy more from you and refer other people to you as long as you offer superior service and a risk-free guarantee?

To me, the answer is obvious. For example, people who purchase my books and tapes directly from me have a lifetime guarantee. If, for any reason, they are ever dissatisfied with their purchase, they can return it to me for a full refund or credit. The only stipulation is that the products are in resalable condition.

Many seminar leaders offer a full money back guarantee if the participant does not feel he or she is getting what was paid for and leaves by a certain time. And, some of these seminar leaders allow the participants to keep the materials from the program. That really is a better than risk-free guarantee.

There are many more examples. The point is to offer a satisfaction guarantee to your customers, and go beyond that by reversing the risk of purchasing as much as possible. Adapt some of the above methods of offering the better than risk-free guarantee. When you communicate this policy to customers and prospects, people will flock to do business with you.

Your Turn   ***Answer the following question:***

▶ How will you adapt risk reversal to your business?

Treat Employees as Customers

In the description of rewards and recognition you learned the importance of noticing and rewarding your employees for outstanding service performances. Doing so will motivate them to continue to demonstrate positive behaviors. It is equally important for you to realize your employees are customers, too. They are your internal customers, and you must treat them with the courtesy and respect you provide to your buying customers.

Too often, I have worked with businesses that had customer service problems, because the same managers or owners who told the employees to provide great service to the customers treated the employees like dirt. You cannot expect employees to provide great service if you do not treat them with the same respect, courtesy and professionalism you expect them to provide to customers. *Remember that your staff will treat customers the way you treat your staff.*

In stark contrast to what many authors, consultants and customer service experts would have us believe, there is a philosophy that states "The Customer Comes Second." The concept has merit for every business. The premise is that employees come first in the company. When employees are treated well, they will treat customers well. This is the philosophy I recommend to everyone. Before you can take care of anyone else or help anyone else accomplish anything, take care of yourself and help yourself.

The bottom line is that you must provide great service to your employees. They, in turn will provide great service to your customers. Then, your bottom line will become bigger.

Your Turn

Answer the following question:

► How do you treat your employees?

Customer Special Events

Special events for your customers are a great way to strengthen relationships. Some companies have special sales for the general public, while others have private sales for their credit card holders. You, too, can create a special event for your best customers.

Host a cocktail party or other social gathering at your place of business after hours. Invite several good customers to dinner at a nice restaurant. Treat them to a round of golf, tickets to a sporting event or show, or do something special for their families. Hold a Customer Appreciation Day.

Special events for customers do not have to be elaborate or expensive. They only have to be special. They have to let your customers know you care about them as people, not just for their business transactions. To find out how you can make them feel special, ask them. Then, wait a short while and give them what they want and like. They will reward you with their loyalty.

Your special events will have another benefit. As your customers network, they will establish new business relationships. As these relationships grow and prosper, your customers will stay loyal to you for an even longer period of time because you demonstrated that you care for their business success, not just your own.

Your Turn

Answer the following question:

▶ What customer special events are appropriate for your business in the next six months? Twelve months?

Strategic Customer Alliances

You will keep more of your customers longer by forming alliances with them. This is not as crazy an idea as it may seem. You do not have to make your customers financial partners in your business. Rather, you make them partners in doing business. Here are a few suggestions:

► SITE VISITS

Invite your customers to spend a day with you at your place of business. Let them go where they please, ask questions of anyone, and even try to work for a while. Ask them to view everything with a critical eye.

Having them on your site can be of tremendous benefit to you. First, it shows them you care enough to invite them into your business. Second, it tells them you think they are important, because you are asking their opinion on how to improve your business. Third, it helps you get an objective opinion from an outsider on how well your business is running.

After you invite customers on site, the next step in creating the strategic alliance is for you to visit your customers. This may be at their place of business, at their homes (depending on how close you are with them) or at a social function. If you want to make a customer a strategic partner, become intimately involved with them. Offer to help them, just as they are helping you. How well do strategic customer alliances work? Just look at the successes of Ford and Mazda, Borland and Wordperfect (before WordPerfect was bought by Novell), AT&T and its many "customer allies/partners." The list goes on.

Do you work with one accountant? Do you have a personal physician? How many financial planners or stock brokers are you working with? How many suppliers are you working with? How long have you been working with these people?

All these relationships are strategic alliances or partnerships. You help these people succeed just as they help you succeed. Shouldn't you do the same thing with your customers? Remember that it is easier and less expensive to do business with a current customer than to acquire a new one. And you will have more current customers if you create more strategic alliances.

► CUSTOMERS AS SALES AGENTS

Customers who perceive themselves as strategic partners for your business become your best sales agents. They will tell others about how great it is to do business with you. They are now more than referral sources. They are advocates and recommenders. They have a stake in helping you succeed. When they refer someone to you, that person comes with a totally different mindset, based on the enthusiasm and passion of your customer advocate.

These new customers will come to you with a positive attitude because you have already been endorsed by someone they trust. It is up to you not to let the new customers down.

On the other hand, customers who are not involved in a strategic alliance with you may not say anything good about you. They may not say anything bad, but they also may not say anything. No reference means no sale for you.

Therefore, try to establish as many strategic alliances as possible. They will help you more than you know. And, even if there is someone who does not become your customer today, plant the seed for a strategic alliance in the future. You will be glad you did.

Your Turn

Answer the following questions that will help you decide which customers should become your strategic partners:

► With whom do I do the majority of my business? *List all the companies or people.*

► What is it they need, want or expect from me?

► Have I determined their perception of my service quality?

_____ Yes   _____ No

► Have I determined their level of customer satisfaction?

_____ Yes   _____ No

► (If you answered Yes to the last two questions) What do I know that my customers need that I can give them?

► Do I have to develop customer service programs before I attempt to create strategic partnerships?

► How can each of my strategic partners and I benefit from working more closely together?

► What obstacles, problems or objections can I foresee when I approach my customer about forming a strategic partnership? (Consider time, money, effort, etc.)

► What types of networked alliances can I help my customers form?

► How will this or these strategic partnerships benefit my other customers?

These questions will help you form strategic partnerships with your customers. The end result will be superior quality in your products and services, improved levels of customer service, and increased levels of customer satisfaction. The end result will be repeat purchases, more referrals, and increased business and profitability for you.

Measuring the Power of Customer Service

Focus passionately on your customers. Do whatever it takes to learn about their needs, wants, expectations and desires. Give them whatever you can that is within your power. Give your employees the training and the authority to do the same.

Measure everything you do within your business, and measure everything you do related to your customers. Get your customers to define quality for you, then measure it. Get them to define superior customer service, give it to them and then measure it accordingly. Get them to tell you how to satisfy them, do it, and then measure it. And, once you have collected all these measurements through some or all of the techniques described in this book, analyze your measurements and find out where you can improve. By continually measuring quality and customer satisfaction, you will become more customer focused, and that will help you be successful.

ASK YOURSELF

► How can customer service be a powerful marketing tool in your business?

► What service marketing programs are best suited for your business? How will you implement each of these programs?

► Describe the type of effort and time commitment you are willing to make to these techniques, to see that they are successful.

CHAPTER SIX

THE

CUSTOMER

AS

RATER

THE CUSTOMER RATES EVERY ENCOUNTER

You need to realize—quickly—that every time you do business with a customer, that customer is rating you. We may not know exactly what standards or criteria a customer is using, but we can be sure of one thing: the customer is rating every encounter as to the level and quality of service, and their own level of satisfaction with the entire interaction.

If you do not think this is true, think about what you do every time you buy something. Do you review the situation and consider how you were greeted, how the salesperson or clerk spoke to you, and how they treated you throughout the entire encounter? You do it, I do it, and your customers do it.

As a business owner, it is your responsibility to have an idea of the criteria that customers use when they rate you and your business. Several years ago, the research firm, Zeithaml, Parasuraman and Berry investigated the parameters customers use to rate businesses during service encounters. Their findings identified ten dimensions of customer service. Subsequent research supports their findings, and re-categorizes it into the five dimensions that customers use to act as a "RATER" of business:

Reliability

Assurance

Tangibility

Empathy

Responsiveness

Let's look at a description of each dimension:

Reliability refers to your ability to perform and live up to your promises. When you promise to deliver something to a customer in some form, you need to do just what you say you are going to do, as dependably and accurately as possible. If a customer calls and you say you will call back in fifteen minutes, do you do that, or does it take a day or two to return the call? If you promise that your invoices to customers will be error-free, do you make sure that you never send out an incorrect invoice? This is the reliability dimension. You do what you say you are going to do, when you say you are going to do it, and you do it right the first time.

Assurance is the knowledge and courtesy of employees, and their ability to convey trust and confidence. Assurance also assumes these attributes:

▶ A competent service provider, who possesses the required skills and knowledge to perform the job well. You know exactly what you are supposed to do for the customer and can do it without fumbling around, making mistakes, or delaying the transaction. You are able to answer any questions the customer may have. You build competence, and also confidence, by providing quality training for yourself and your employees.

Tangibility relates to the appearance of the physical facility, the equipment, the staff and any communication materials your business may use. How the business looks is very important, because customer service is intangible and it is used at the time it is provided. How the business and the people who provide the customer service look is judged as positive or negative by the customer. This concept was introduced in Chapter Four, *Making Customer Service Work*, as one of the skills that employees need to develop to provide excellent customer service.

Empathy is the caring and individualized attention provided to customers. Empathy also assumes these attributes:

▶ Customers want you and your employees to be easily accessible. They want to be able to approach you when they need you. You need to be available to them to provide great customer service when they need it—not just when it is convenient for you. If you are not available, your competitors will be, and your customers will become their customers. Access refers to your staying open later in the evening, opening on weekends or holidays, opening earlier in the morning, and conducting business when your customers want to meet with you.

► Communication in customer service can make or break a customer's perception of your business. I personally believe that communication is the cause of all success between people, as well as the source of all disagreements and failures. When two people communicate, things work out; when they do not, we have problems. How well do you keep customers informed of what is going on, in a language they understand? How well do you listen to customers? Do you explain things and make certain the customer has a grasp of what you say?

► Understanding the customer is vital to your success. You have to know your customers intimately. Do what it takes to get information about the customer, including likes, dislikes, hobbies, friends, needs, wants, expectations, birthdays, family members, and anything else that might help you establish a relationship with that customer. Where your regular customers are concerned, make sure you recognize them when they come in, and use their names correctly. Find out what their specific objectives are for doing business with you. Determine exactly what they want to achieve. Let them know that you understand them well and you still want to get to know them better.

Responsiveness refers to your willingness to help customers, or the willingness of your employees to do the same. Do you provide prompt service when the customer requires it? Do you resolve problems or complaints quickly and to the customer's total and complete satisfaction? If you schedule an appointment, are you there at the appropriate time? The answers to questions like these determine how responsive you are to your customers.

Your Turn   ***Answer the following question:***
► How does each dimension apply to your business?

Customers rate you either consciously or subconsciously on these five dimensions. How are you doing on these subjective ratings? What will you do to improve your performance in each area?

Don't think it is sufficient if you are doing well in two or three areas. There is always another competitor who does well in all five areas, and this competitor will soon get your customers. If customers do not rate you high in these areas, and if you have not made financial or psychological switching costs too high for them, they will go elsewhere. Sometimes, customers will leave you simply because you were not giving them what they wanted in one area, not necessarily all five—and, all you had to do was ask.

ASK YOURSELF

► Use this chart to evaluate yourself on each of the five customer rating dimensions.

1. Identify how your customers define each of the five service factors. Write the definition in the space below the factor.

2. Determine what real-world experiences have detracted from the service experience for your customers. Also determine those experiences that have met customer expectations and those that have exceeded customer expectations (service enhancers).

   Write those descriptions in the appropriate boxes.

3. Compare this analysis with information you receive from your customer surveys or other customer information sources.

Service Factors	Service Detractors	Standard Expectations	Service Enhancers
Reliability			
Assurance			
Tangibles			
Empathy			
Responsiveness			

► Compare your opinion of your customer service with your customers' opinions.

CHAPTER
SEVEN

MEASURING
CUSTOMER
SATISFACTION

CUSTOMER SERVICE RESEARCH METHODS

Methods of customer service are internal to your company or organization. You must also go outside your company's boundaries and determine the service needs and satisfaction levels of your customers. You can do this through a variety of research methods and data-collection techniques.

Secondary Data

Secondary data is information that has been collected for some other purpose than the one you are currently investigating. Sources of secondary data include information you already have within your company, as well as information you can get from stock reports, trade publications, research organizations, census data and any other providers of information.

For example, if you are interested in what type of customers in your industry buy the most of your product or register the most complaints, you can ask your trade association for information on purchaser characteristics or profiles of complaining customers. This information may be available through warranty information or from research conducted for some other reason, and the trade association may be able to provide it for you. That is secondary data. You have not collected it yourself to research a particular problem or situation; however, you are able to use the information to support another project.

Secondary data provides both cost and time economies. The information is already available and it is usually free, especially if you gather it from your local library. The disadvantages are that the data may not directly fit your customer service situation, the data may be obsolete by the time you use it, and it may not be accurate enough for you to make informed decisions about improving customer service.

Consider your secondary data with care as you relate it to customer service and satisfaction levels. However, always use secondary data—it can help you develop a better focus on your primary data-collection methods.

Primary Data

Primary data is information you collect yourself, which is directly related to your research project. For example, you may be trying to identify areas for improvement in your customer service system.

While primary data collection is much more accurate than secondary data, because it relates specifically to the customer research you are conducting, it is also much more expensive. You can collect primary data through a number of means including, but not limited to, experiments, surveys, questionnaires, interviews, and opinion polls. You can use primary data to determine people's attitudes, opinions, preferences, behaviors and personalities.

Primary data collection can be used to classify your current customers into demographic, psychographic and sociographic categories. This helps you to more accurately determine the profile of the people responding to your inquiries. For example, if you know that your male customers with incomes over $35,000 make more purchases of your product or service than female customers in the same income bracket, you can target your marketing efforts in this direction. You can also determine the satisfaction levels of both groups, and if the female group is less satisfied, you can conduct additional research to learn these reasons and then develop programs, products or services to increase the satisfaction level of this customer group.

You can collect primary data either through communication or observation techniques. Communication means surveys and interviews requiring direct involvement of the customer, and observation means simply watching the customers' behaviors. Both of these techniques are valid methods of data collection.

Qualitative Research

Qualitative research attempts to subjectively understand the experience of customers when they purchase or use your product or service. There are no hard measurements with qualitative research. You collect information on customer service and satisfaction levels through observation, interviews, focus groups and personal experience (where you act as your own customer).

Even though it is difficult to quantify this type of information, you can gain tremendous insight into what your customers think about your quality and service. Usually, customers will be more than happy to tell you their perceptions, thoughts and feelings about your product or service. You must then compile and collate this information so that you can use it to determine ways to improve your service quality and customer satisfaction ratings.

Quantitative Research

Quantitative research is objective and measurable. You collect information according to some predetermined standard, such as a five- or seven-point scale, using a questionnaire or survey. The survey can be written, oral or conducted over the telephone. When you complete your research, you can perform statistical analyses on the data to determine your customer satisfaction ratings and your customers' ratings of your service quality.

Sampling

Sampling is a determination of how many customers you will research to get the information you are seeking. There is no ideal sample size for a given research project, unless of course you can survey or interview every customer you do business with. Unfortunately, this is not practical or feasible, so you must research a representative sample. Statistics books will tell you how to determine the exact sample size for your project. For most purposes, if you can research 50 to 100 people (or more) at a given time, you probably have a representative sample.

You can increase the power of your research and sample by randomly selecting the customers you want to survey or interview. Random selection means just what it says. You pick the people at random without any predetermining factors. Again, for more information, consult a research methods or statistics book.

Research Design: An Example

Here is an example of a customer satisfaction research project. It is simple, yet extremely effective in gathering the information a company needs.

Category	Description
Objective	To determine customer satisfaction levels of training programs
Time Period	July–December, 1995
Sample	All purchasers, male and female: minimum 100 subjects
Format	Written survey with scaled responses
Analysis	Percentages, histograms and Pareto charts
Data Collection Time	January, 1996
Report	Distributed to all employees
Follow up	Work to improve areas of service quality that need attention as determined by the survey

Fill in your own descriptions for each category.

Category	Description
Objective	_____
Time Period	_____
Sample	_____
Format	_____
Analysis	_____
Data Collection Time	_____
Report	_____
Follow up	_____

This outline gives you a format to follow when you conduct your customer research. The tools you can use to conduct this research are described in the next section.

QUESTIONNAIRES AND SURVEYS

Most customer service and satisfaction research is conducted by survey. Surveys can be written or oral questionnaires, telephone or face-to-face interviews, and focus groups.

The survey method is by far the most common data collection technique. Surveys usually consist of several questions or statements along with associated responses that require people to answer according to some predefined scale. Some surveys allow people to answer in an open-ended manner, thereby describing their responses in greater detail. Both response methods are useful and provide excellent information about customer satisfaction levels.

Surveys are typically self-report mechanisms in which the customer answers the questions for himself or herself. Sometimes, other people respond for the customer. In either case, the idea is to get the customer to provide the most accurate answers to your questions so that you can evaluate your service quality, customer service efforts, and levels of customer satisfaction.

One special type of survey is called an *intercept*. Here, a researcher stops a customer as they enter or leave a place of business and begins to ask them questions—the customer is "intercepted." The intercept technique can be a written survey, an oral interview, or both.

Format and Layout

You can choose from numerous formats and layouts for your surveys. The key is to keep the survey "user friendly," easy to understand and to respond to. Do not make your survey too long, as people will lose interest in an extensive survey, especially if you have "intercepted" them to get their responses.

If you mail out the survey to your customers, you have a better chance of them completing a lengthy questionnaire than if you stop them in person. People perceive they have more time at home or at the office and, if they are interested in your business, they will take the time to complete your survey.

When you develop the survey, format it so questions that are easiest to answer are at the beginning. This important technique gives the customer a feeling of accomplishment and a sense of comfort with the survey. Sometimes, the first few "giveaway" questions are simple, open-ended questions that get the respondent into writing and thinking about the survey. Here are three questions you can use or modify for the beginning of your survey:

1. What reason did you have for shopping with us (or buying from us) today?

2. Have you purchased from us before?

3. Did you find everything you were looking for?

These simple, open-ended and yes/no questions get the customer into the habit of responding.

Also consider the format and layout. Do you want the questions to be followed with a leader (. . . .) on the same line as the answers? Or, do you want the answers placed below the questions? The choice is yours. Surveys have been successful at obtaining information using both formats. Here is what both formats look like.

---

1. How satisfied were you with the service you received from our staff. . . .

	Dissatisfied	Somewhat		Very Satisfied
	1	2	3	4	5

OR,

1. How satisfied were you with the service you received from our staff?

Dissatisfied	Somewhat	Very Satisfied
1	2	3

Decide what format and layout works best for you and your customers. You may want to test both and determine which surveys with a particular format receive more responses and returns.

Question Construction

Successful surveys ask the questions they are supposed to ask. Only one thought, attribute or skill is rated in each question.

For example, asking a customer "Was the staff courteous and friendly?" does not give you information you can use. What are you trying to get at: courtesy or friendliness? And, when the answer is yes or no, which attribute are they responding to—courtesy or friendliness? If you are trying to find out about either courtesy or friendliness, or both, ask separate questions for each.

The most important characteristic when you construct survey questions is to make sure the questions are simple and direct with only one thought or item per question. Ask enough questions to get all the information you want from your customers and to be able to determine their level of satisfaction with you, what you sell, and the service you provide.

Survey Question Responses

Responses to questions are either open-ended or closed-ended, the latter usually being a rating of some kind. When you look at a survey, you can immediately tell the response being called for by the first word of the question or statement. If a question or statement begins with What, Where, Who, Why, Describe, Tell or List, it is an open-ended question and requires a descriptive or subjective answer; if a question begins with Did, How, or Were or a pronoun, a closed-ended response is usually required. While there are times when questions or statements can begin with any of these words and be the opposite of the norm, the majority of the time these classifications hold true.

To measure customer service performance and customer satisfaction, you need "hard" data, which comes from measurements. Therefore, scale your responses to each question, and try to use the same scale whenever and wherever possible within the same survey.

Scales are typically ordinal, where the answers ranges from "Poor to Excellent," with one, two or three other possible responses in between. This is acceptable. Unfortunately, when we use these scales, we put numbers on them, such as 1 through 5, and then analyze the numbers. Ordinal data do not have true numerical intervals and should not be analyzed in this way. However, most managers tend to do this and it has become accepted practice among customer service researchers to analyze this type of data as if it were truly numerical. So, if you are measuring your satisfaction levels using category descriptions and then converting them to numbers, go ahead, even if it makes research and statistical purists cringe.

Your scales should always allow a neutral point for the respondent. You do this by including an odd number of possible responses, such as 3, 5 or 7. When you are working with percentages, you may want to use a 10 or 100 point scale. Even if you use different types of scales in the same survey, do not mix the analysis of the scales.

The most widely used types of scales in customer service and satisfaction surveys are illustrated on page 164.

For any of the rating scales and their descriptive terms, you can substitute satisfied and dissatisfied for the responses, or some wording about meeting, not meeting and exceeding expectations. Word your questions so the responses make sense to the customer.

Telephone Surveys

Telephone surveys can be highly effective in gathering data if the surveyor is well trained in asking the survey questions, has a script to follow, and calls customers at a convenient time. The advantage of telephone surveys over written (mailed) surveys and questionnaires is that an experienced surveyor (customer service representative or telemarketer) can focus on what the respondent is saying and gear open-ended questions to particular responses and elicit more information. The surveyor can also make deter-

3 POINT SCALE

1	2	3
Poor	Fair	Excellent

4 POINT SCALE (used but not highly recommended)

1	2	3	4
Poor	Fair	Good	Excellent

5 POINT SCALE

1	2	3	4	5
Poor	Fair	Neutral	Good	Excellent
(Well Below Expectations)	(Below Expectations)	(Meets Expectations)	(Above Expectations)	(Far Exceeds Expectations)

7 POINT SCALE (also known as Likert-type scale)

1	2	3	4	5	6	7
Very Poor (Dissatisfied)	Poor	Somewhat Poor	Neutral	Somewhat Good	Good	Very Good (Satisfied)

10 POINT SCALE (Add a 0 point to make it an 11 point scale)

1	2	3	4	5	6	7	8	9	10
Not At All Important									Extremely Important

100 (101) POINT SCALE

0% ———————————————————————————— 100%
Complete Dissatisfaction   Complete Satisfaction

minations from the respondent's tone of voice regarding the veracity of the answers.

The main disadvantage of telephone surveys is that the respondent can hang up at any time, or may never even talk to the surveyor. Also, you are not always able to reach someone at home or at the office to interview them.

Telephone surveys are an excellent tool to either support or replace written surveys. In appropriate instances, they can be used as your sole data collection technique. To make sure your telephone surveys are successful, follow these five principles.

1. **Keep the survey simple.**

   Since the respondent is listening to the questions or statements, make them and the response scales easy to understand. Complex questions, multiple answers or confusing response scales have no place in a telephone survey. Show appreciation for customers who respond to your telephone survey by not taking too much of their time or confusing them.

2. **Have a script.**

   Give all your telephone surveyors a script to follow. The script should contain information about how they introduce themselves when the customer answers the phone, how they ask each question, how they respond to customer questions, what to do when a customer goes off on a tangent with an answer, how to keep a customer on the line to complete the survey and how to thank the customer for helping you. Make sure everyone follows the script to the letter. This is not a telemarketing sales script. It is a customer service research script. You must always do everything the same way to preserve the integrity of the data.

3. **Make the response form easy to work with.**

   Your surveyors must be able to record a customer's response to a question very quickly and then be able to move on to the next question. The response form must be easy for the surveyor to work with and follow, so that they never place a response in the wrong column or next to a different question than the one for which it was intended.

   The format and layout for your telephone surveys should have the question along the top and the responses flush right in a column. This will minimize, and hopefully negate, any possibility of a mistake on your surveyor's part.

Here is an example of the telephone interview survey and response form.

---

1. How satisfied were you with the service you received from the front desk staff?

Very Dissatisfied	1
Somewhat Dissatisfied	2
It was O.K	3
Somewhat Satisfied	4
Very Satisfied	5

Your telephone surveyor simply circles the response the customer gives, and since the responses are "way off to the right," there should be no cause for confusion or problems. With a telephone survey, keep the response key or scales the same for each question. (This holds true for written surveys as well.) While it is true you can provide new instructions to the respondent, or on a written survey the person can read the instructions related to the new response scales, it is easier for everyone if you use one scale throughout the survey.

Again, remember that there is no true right or wrong here. I am advocating elegant simplicity, especially if you have minimal experience with surveys and research.

4. **Train your surveyors.**

This alone will make or break a telephone survey. A survey can be great—properly worded, easy to use with an excellent response form. The script can be simple to follow, and the customer can be ready to respond. However, if your surveyors are not trained in how to communicate and administer the survey as well as record responses, there will definitely be problems. Train them extensively, and do not let them call a customer until you are satisfied that they have interviewed you and several other people appropriately.

5. **Thank the customer, even before the surveyor starts the survey.**

   This may seem a little out of place in steps to making a telephone survey successful. On the contrary, saying thank you at the beginning when the customer agrees to the survey, saying thank you during the survey after every few questions, and definitely saying thank you when the customer completes the survey will make your data collection easier, more effective, and give you a more accurate picture of how well you are serving and satisfying your customers. Customers who perceive you care about them trust you and are more likely to give you honest answers.

Analyzing the Telephone Survey

After you collect all the data, conduct the same types of statistical analyses on the telephone survey data as you would on written survey responses. You can also combine the results of telephone and written surveys and then subject them to analysis. An interesting point may be to classify the responses according to how the data were collected to see if there are any differences in your customers' perceptions, based on whether they responded in writing (self-report) or by telephone.

Consider Scheduling Interviews

Telephone surveys, like face-to-face interviews, require a time investment on the part of the customer. Therefore, you may want to think about scheduling a telephone interview appointment with the customer, just as you would if you were going to interview the customer in person. You may find that the customer is much more appreciative and receptive to you since you show concern for his or her valuable time. You may even get more information from the customer than you were looking for in the survey. Think about how you feel when your telephone rings at dinner time and someone wants to ask you just a few questions; you're really not that receptive. Telephone survey appointments will not always get a customer to agree to respond to you, but consider this option.

Personal Interviews

Personal interviews can be either structured or unstructured. Structured interviews require that you ask specific questions of your customer in a particular order. You do not deviate, and if the customer goes off on a tangent, you try to bring him or her back to the issue at hand.

If you have never conducted a *structured interview*, you should first develop a script describing the introduction and purpose of the interview along with instructions for how you will ask questions. Include the response scale that people will use when answering. List the questions to be asked, plus some expected responses. If customers will be allowed to answer in a qualitative or subjective manner, tell them that at the beginning. When a customer answers your question, mark the response directly on your form. If the answer is not one that you expected, write it down as close to verbatim as possible. You may even want to record the session to make sure you do not miss any important information.

Unstructured interviews are highly subjective in nature and the customer is allowed to respond in almost a free-associative manner. You ask certain questions and see where the interview goes. Of course, you can ask specific questions during an unstructured interview, as you would in a structured one, and I recommend it. However you do it, you must be able to record the customer's responses. If you are not a fast writer, audio tape or video tape the interview.

Another excellent use of the personal interview is to validate written or telephone surveys. After you receive these responses, call some of the customers and invite them in for a personal interview. Speak with them one-on-one and try to identify an even deeper level of their feelings related to customer service and satisfaction. Again, record their responses and never forget to say thank you.

You may want to interview several people at one time. That is fine, and it brings us to the concept of focus groups.

Focus Groups

Focus groups are groups of five to ten people (customers), who meet with a facilitator to answer questions related to a company's performance and to describe their satisfaction with the company's products or services. Focus groups are used extensively in market research. Their value is sometimes limited to the specific group of respondents in attendance. To validate your focus group information, conduct several different groups with customers from different service areas, with different purchasing habits, and who have different perceptions about your service quality and their level of satisfaction.

A focus group should be run by an outside facilitator who has experience in administering these types of group interviews. If you lead them yourself, there is a tendency to bias the responses. So, invest the money and have someone from the outside help you. You will be more confident in your results when the facilitator has no stake in them.

Record the focus group, at least on audio tape if not both audio and video. Play it back several times to gather pieces of information you may otherwise miss. Then, prepare a report on the participants' comments and thoughts.

Although focus groups tend to be more subjective and open-ended than written surveys, you can ask the customers to respond to specific questions with scaled response items. This will allow you to compare their responses directly with those you receive on the surveys.

Be careful of the *beneficent respondent* in your focus group. This is the person who will always give the answers he or she thinks you want to hear. While it may be a boost to your ego and a pat on your company's back to hear you are doing such a great job in serving and satisfying your customers, this may actually be false information. Compare this person's responses with the rest of the focus group and against any written surveys you may have. Also, if this person has completed a written survey, or if you think the person may be a beneficent respondent, ask him or her to complete a survey, then compare the written responses with the oral ones. If they match, you have to dig further for the truth. If they do not match, you probably have a bias in your focus group data.

One other thing about focus groups. People are sometimes hesitant to participate in a focus group, but are very willing to be part of a "Customer Advisory Forum" or a "Customer Council." You can call it whatever you like. Determine which name your customers feel most comfortable with, call the group by that name, and you may be able to increase participation in the focus group for your research program.

ASK YOURSELF

► Identify the customer satisfaction measurement systems you have in place.

► Explain how you can use customer feedback to improve your customer service.

► What is the most effective type of data collection tool for your business?

► How will you develop a more effective data collection tool?

CHAPTER EIGHT

KEEPING

CUSTOMERS

FOR

LIFE

THE KEY TO LONG-LASTING SUCCESS

I have said this several times throughout the book: your only purpose for being in business is to get and keep customers. Without customers, you have no business. You have to gear everything you do to finding out exactly what your customers need, want and expect from you, and then giving them all that and more.

Once you secure them as customers, do everything possible to keep them. We have already talked about a variety of methods to create customer commitment and sustain customer loyalty. Reward and recognition programs, thank you notes, newsletters, customer councils, and various other programs and techniques will all work in your favor.

Yet, it seems that whatever you do is never quite enough. Someone, somewhere, always comes up with a new and better way to service customers. And, your customers start asking you when they will receive those products or services, or something comparable. You, of course, want to do everything in your power to give them what they want. But, it just may not be possible. I suggest you figure out a way to serve the customer. Who knows, you might get a customer for life. Let's see how this might work.

Several years ago, I hired a landscape company to take care of my front and back yards. I wanted trees, colorful plants, border plants, mulch, and some landscape design. The company was very accommodating; they did an excellent job at a fair price. I definitely received value for my money, and they completed the project within a reasonable time.

When I asked the company if they also provided lawn maintenance services, such as mowing and trimming the bushes, they said they did, for a fee of $60 a month. I were currently paying only $50 a month, and I was looking to change service companies. Here was a chance for the landscape company to acquire my monthly business, and keep in touch with me about upgrading my landscaping on a regular basis. The company owner refused to lower his price, even though I just spent several thousand dollars with him. When I asked him to reconsider, he became indignant and said if he knew I was going to ask him to match someone else's price, he never would have done the landscaping in the first place.

Needless to say, he did not get my lawn maintenance business, and he never got any other business or referrals from me again. The landscaper had an opportunity to acquire a pre-qualified, already satisfied customer for a long period of time. He had the potential to tap into this customer's network of referrals. He had just completed one large business transaction with this customer, and all he had to do was take a lesser profit on another transaction to guarantee himself ongoing and volume business.

Your Turn

Answer the following questions:

► What would you have done in your business?

► Would you match the previous provider's price to acquire a customer and gain all the benefits of the long-term relationship?

► If the price was below your cost for the product or service, would you try to negotiate?

► Would you even consider taking the business at cost to secure the customer and reap the tangential benefits that the relationship would create?

CUSTOMER RETENTION STRATEGIES AND TACTICS

Here are fifty ways you can keep customers for life. Do what you must to make them work for your business. Adapt them as you see fit. Just make sure you implement as many of these recommendations as possible on a daily basis. When you do, you will retain customers for life, and turn them into recommenders and advocates.

Fifty Ways to Keep Your Customers for Life

1. Create a Service Oriented Culture

Everyone in the company must be customer service oriented. All employees must realize that they work for the customer, and their job is to ensure the ultimate satisfaction of the customer. Everything else they do must support their efforts to serve and satisfy customers.

2. Have a Service Vision

A vision is vital to the service success of any organization. A vision is more than just a philosophy of doing business. The vision must be the corporate cultural ethic. Everyone must believe and live the vision for your company to provide excellent customer service and keep customers for life. Management may develop the vision, but the staff must make it a reality. The service vision must be an extension of the company mission statement, and must be supported by company and personal values.

3. Commit to Total Support

True success comes from total organizational support. The owner or top management may decide to embark on a customer service program, but line employees implement the program. If these people do not support the initiative, the program will not work. Total support is needed.

4. Put Policies in Writing

Put your service policies in writing to benefit both your customers and your employees. This way, there will be no mistakes or misunderstandings. Be aware, however, that your employees should have the authority to grant discretionary exceptions to the policies when the need arises. Remember, policies are guidelines—not laws—and they must remain flexible.

5. Design Flexibility into Your Service Policies

Keep your policies flexible, because each customer and situation is different. Your employees must know they can modify a written or stated policy to ensure the customer's total satisfaction at any given moment, and you *must* support your employees' decisions and actions in these situations.

6. Empower Employee

Give your employees the authority to go with their responsibility of satisfying and keeping the customer. Allow them to make decisions on the spot and support those decisions. Remember, their job is to satisfy the customers and keep them coming back. Employees should not have to look for you or a manager every time a customer needs something, even if it is out of the ordinary.

7. Train Your Employees to Do It Right the First Time

Repair, rework and additional free services are very costly. Doing it right the first time guarantees greater profitability, happier customers and more long-term customers. If you must do something over again for a customer, do it even "righter" the second time.

8. Invest in Employee Training

Train, train and then retrain to retain your employees. Give them on-the-job training, off-the-job training, tapes, books, seminars, workshops, anything that will help them do their jobs better. While you may find qualified people who have just graduated from school, nothing prepares a person better for handling customers than the training they receive on the job and in practically applied programs. Ideally, you should pay for some or all of their training, including paid time off to attend outside sessions.

9. Market the Service Program

All of your marketing should communicate that you provide superior customer service, are interested only in total customer satisfaction, and will do everything possible to keep your customers. The message must be stated in everything you send out to the public and the trades. And, it must be backed up by the behaviors of you and your staff.

10. Hire Good People; Hire Nice People

Hire people who are good and well qualified. Innate people skills go a long way toward helping your staff provide superior customer service and retain your customers. You can always train people to perform technical skills; you cannot train goodness and niceness.

11. Do Not Make Customers Pay for Service

Pay for everything related to customer service, including shipping charges on returns, long distance telephone calls, postage, and anything else the customer is normally charged. If you do not pay for the cost of service, your competition will, and then your customers will become their customers.

12. Reward Loyalty

What gets rewarded gets done. If you reward both customers and employees for their loyalty, they both will stay with you for a long time. The rewards must be perceived as valuable by the recipient, but they do not have to cost you much money. To find out what people perceive as valuable, ask them.

13. Set Standards of Performance

Let everyone know exactly what they must do to provide superior customer service. Make these standards as objective and measurable as possible, even though you may provide an intangible service. When people achieve these performance levels, customer retention, satisfaction and loyalty naturally follow.

14. Inspect What You Expect

What gets measured gets done. Measure the performance of your staff members and you will see an increase in performance levels, quality and productivity. You will also ultimately see an increase in profitability. Sometimes, performance improves simply because people believe they are going to be measured. Personal improvement becomes a self-fulfilling prophesy.

15. Cross Train

Train your employees in other people's jobs. They will be able to provide more assistance to customers, more assistance to each other, and you will become less dependent on "irreplaceable" employees when they are not at work.

16. Trade Jobs

Have your employees work in other departments. They will develop an appreciation for what other people in the company do, and therefore no employee will blame another for a customer problem. In fact, since the employees have experience in other areas, they will be able to solve more problems and satisfy more customers on the spot. Then, when a problem or a complaint comes in, everyone or anyone can own it and take care of it.

17. Set Up Easily Accessible Service Systems

Make your customer service systems easy for customers to access. Have them reach a person on the telephone as soon as they call in, or have them speak with an employee who can help them as soon as they arrive at your place of business. Do not make it hard for customers to come to you. They may decide not to do business with you again. Try to stay away from Automatic Call Distribution phone systems. When customers call, they want to talk to a person, not listen to a computer.

18. Create User Friendly Service Systems

Make your customer service systems easy to use. The customer is the reason for your business, not someone who is in the way of doing business. Make the customers feel and know they can bring a problem to your attention, voice a complaint, get it resolved as quickly as possible and receive superb treatment during all their contacts with your company.

19. Educate the Customer

Do not assume the customer knows what you know. Use every customer contact as a chance to educate the customer about something related to your business. Even if you are just educating them about your great return policy, teach them. They will be appreciative and show their appreciation by continuing to do business with you.

20. Handle Complaints Properly

Acknowledge that the customer is upset, listen carefully, assure them you are doing everything possible at this moment to resolve their complaint, and then resolve the complaint. Then, when they express appreciation for your efforts, use the opportunity to increase their loyalty. Thank them for bringing the problem to your attention, apologize again for the problem, and try to sell them something else.

21. Turn Complaints into Additional Sales

The customer is most receptive to continuing to do business with you after you resolve a complaint. Using this opportunity to make a sale is both ethical and practical. Your customers will appreciate your interest in them. They will probably buy from you now and go out and tell their friends how well and quickly you handled their problem. You will develop a reputation with customers of credibility, reliability and honesty. Plus, you will increase your profitability, because the cost of this sale is virtually $0.

22. Realize That Every Customer Has A Lifetime Value

When a customer buys from you, that purchase is not a one time, one price deal. Consider the potential that customer brings to your business. How much money could that customer spend with you over a lifetime? That amount is the lifetime value of a customer and that is the *type and level of service they should receive every time* they do business with you.

23. Beg for Customer Feedback

It is not enough to send out surveys or leave comment cards at the cash register. You must get as much customer feedback as possible, even if you have to beg for it. If customers are asked their opinion and see that you have implemented their suggestions, they will not only continue to do business with you, they will recommend that friends come to you also. Do whatever you can to solicit their opinions and comments, and then act on their suggestions.

24. Identify Customer Values, Beliefs and Standards

Your service programs must be geared to the values, beliefs, and standards of your customers. If customer values and your values conflict, invite your customers into the business for a discussion to find out why the difference exists and what can be done about it. Then decide if you must modify your position to maintain customer satisfaction and loyalty. However, you should never compromise your ethics and values to satisfy a customer.

25. Get and Use Employee Ideas

Employees, who have daily contact with customers, know more about what customers need, want and expect than you or any other manager could ever hope to know. Get feedback from your employees, listen carefully to their suggestions, and implement as many as possible. Research shows that the best service companies not only get more ideas from their employees, they use more of them. This makes employees feel appreciated and cared about and shows them that you think as much of your internal customers as you do your external customers.

26. Be Fair and Consistent

Customers may not always like or agree with what you do for them, but as long as you treat each one fairly and consistently, they will respect you for it. Consistency enhances your credibility and reliability which are essential for building loyalty and retaining customers.

27. Underpromise and Overdeliver

Customers' expectations can be unrealistically raised when businesses overpromise and underdeliver. Usually, the business cannot meet these expectations, and the customer goes away disappointed. If you set realistic expectations for the customer on your quality and level of service and then exceed those expectations, the customer is more than satisfied. Remember, though, that you should not underpromise to the extent that you insult your customers. They will see through you in a minute and take their business elsewhere.

28. Compete on Benefits, not Products or Prices

Customers can always find another product at a lower price, somehow, somewhere. Always remind your customers of the benefits of doing business with you. Features can be found in every product, but benefits are unique to the way you do business.

Your Turn

To determine the unique benefits of your product or service:

► List its features.

► Write down what purchasing that product/service will do for the customer.

► Write down how it will improve the customer's life.

---

29. Use High Touch not High Tech

High tech gets people to say "Wow!", but it does not get people to care about other people. Your business needs high touch to survive. Stay close to your customers. Get to know them well. The closer you are to your customers, the longer they will do business with you. After all, when you show you care, you become like one of their family. Do whatever it takes to make all your customers part of your family, too.

30. Ask Customers What They Want

Constantly ask your customers what they want from you, what you can do for them and how you can do it better. They may want a new product or service, extended hours, or just something minor that will make them happier. You will never know unless you ask. After you ask, you must give them what they want. They will reward your generosity with loyalty.

31. Manage Service Daily

Every employee in every department is involved in providing superior service to achieve the ultimate goal—keeping the customer for life. Do everything possible to make everyone's job easier so that it will be easier for them to give the customers what they want. If there is a problem during the day, make the necessary adjustments and resolve it quickly. And try to resolve it behind the scenes so all else continues to run smoothly.

32. Know the Cost of Losing a Customer

All employees should know the lifetime value of a customer, the cost of losing even one, and the effect that loss can have on your business. Consider rewarding your employees if they retain your customers over a longer-than-average time period. After all, you are benefiting from the increased number of sales and profits. How about sharing the wealth?

33. Know Your Competition

What kinds of customer services are your competitors providing? What are they doing to retain their customers? Are they offering more benefits, better service policies, or are they just being nicer to the customers? Find out, and if they are doing something you are not doing, then do it. If it works for them, it will probably work for you. Then, go them one better.

34. Conduct Market Research

You can never have enough information about your customers. Do surveys, interviews, whatever it takes to find out what the marketplace wants. Then, adapt your business accordingly. Information is only power when you know how to use it.

35. Conduct Internal Assessments

Constantly evaluate your company's customer service, satisfaction and retention programs and policies. Interview your employees, have them fill out questionnaires, ask your customers at the point of purchase how you are doing, and use this information to improve your service and retention efforts.

36. Know What Your Customers Need, Want and Expect

Businesses run into problems when they think customers need, want or expect one thing, and they really require another. These gaps in perceptions about service delivery ultimately disappoint customers. Find out what customers need, want and expect; then, give it to them and then some.

37. Find, Nurture and Display Customer Champions

Every business has one, two or several employees who are true customer champions. Find out who these people are, nurture and support them, and make them role models for everyone else to follow. Reward their behavior. The rest of your staff will upgrade their service performance to this level to receive similar rewards. The result is a highly motivated, service-oriented staff and a group of satisfied and loyal customers.

38. Practice Effective Communication

Every problem between people is the result of poor communication. Train your people to develop effective communication skills: how to listen first, how to speak so others will listen, how to understand others before trying to be understood, how to receive and give feedback, and how to develop rapport with customers.

39. Use Rapport to Communicate Effectively

The technical skills of communication can be acquired and used, but without rapport there is no communication. The skills of developing rapport can be taught and your employees should learn them. When employees and customers have rapport, there is a feeling of trust and a desire to continue to do business.

40. Smile

Smiling is important when serving a customer. Smiles will usually get a smile in return, but smiles will not guarantee quality customer service. Smiling must be something employees do because it makes them feel good, and it makes the customers feel good.

41. Make Customers Feel Important

The more important you make customers feel, the better they will feel about doing business with you. Call them by name, ask them to tell you about themselves and ask questions about their accomplishments. Your reward will be a lifetime customer.

42. Promote Your Customers

With their permission, of course, use your customers in your marketing and promotion efforts. Let them tell their story to other customers and prospects. These third party endorsements foster tremendous credibility, and your customers will love being involved. Testimonials attract new customers faster than any other technique.

43. Create a Customer Council

Your customer council, like a board of directors or focus group, should meet regularly to scrutinize your business and the service you provide. The council makes suggestions on which you act. You might want to call this a customer advisory board.

44. Market Frequent Buyer Programs

To get your customers excited about doing business with you, start a reward program for frequent buyers. You can use coupons, punch cards, or anything else that helps you keep track of customer activity. When a customer's purchases or referrals reach a certain level, reward him or her with a gift—a deep discount coupon, a free product or service or something more expensive, such as a trip.

45. Accept Only Excellence

If you expect average performance and service, that is what you will get. Therefore, set your expectations high. Accept only excellent performance from your employees, and train your staff to achieve these levels of performance. Good enough should never be good enough.

46. Treat Your Employees As Customers

Employees are your internal customers, your first line of customers, and each of them has a customer somewhere in the value chain. Each employee must provide excellent customer service to every other employee so that they all can provide superior service to customers. This is the only way to guarantee customer satisfaction and retention.

47. Let Customers Know You Care

Send them thank you cards, holiday cards and anything else you can to show them you care. Never let them forget your name. Teach them that whenever they need something, they can come to you for it because you care. Spend time and money marketing your caring attitude to your customers.

48. Make Service Results Visible

Visibility enhances credibility, and credibility is only enhanced by improved performance. Post your customer comment cards and letters for all customers to see. Create a testimonial book for customers to read. Post employees' performance results in their lounge or locker room. Make service results visible so that your employees will constantly improve and your customers will be the beneficiaries of this improved service.

49. Go the Extra Mile

When customers want something from you, give it to them. Then, do something extra. They will be grateful and you will have a long-term customer.

50. Combine Marketing and Customer Service

All of your marketing efforts should communicate your customer service message. In today's competitive marketplace, the thing that differentiates companies is the level and quality of their customer service, and this is the major criteria people use to decide whether or not to continue purchasing from that company. Customer service is a very effective and powerful marketing tool, and marketing is a very effective and powerful customer service tool. Combined, the two will help you keep your customers for life.

Bonus Tip: *Create a Better-Than-Risk-Free Guarantee.*

Let customers know that you are taking the entire risk related to their doing business with you. If they have to return something they purchased, give them a refund, plus a free gift for their troubles. This makes doing business with you a better-than-risk-free proposition for the customer.

Now, Review Everything You Are Doing and Make It Better

Whatever you are doing now to service and satisfy your customers may not be sufficient to keep them tomorrow. A competitor will offer superior customer service on a better product at a lower price that has more benefits. You have to stay one step ahead of your competitors. You must know what they are doing and how they are doing it. Review your customer service policy, then do whatever it takes to make it better.

Remember, you are in business to make money, and the only way you will make money is to have satisfied customers who keep coming back.

CUSTOMER ADVOCATES AND RECOMMENDERS

Now that you know a multitude of ways to keep customers for life and to outservice your competition, strive for an even higher goal where your customers are concerned. Turn your satisfied, loyal and committed customers into advocates and recommenders.

Advocates are customers who go out and talk about you on their own. They do not necessarily refer people to you. They are just out telling the world about how great you treat them, how wonderful it is to do business with you, and how you are the best thing since chicken soup.

You need advocates. They counterbalance any dissatisfied customer who wants to tell ten to twenty other people about his or her negative experience with you. Advocates can tell those same people how wonderful you really are and possibly overcome any negative influence.

Recommenders are people who agree to allow others to call them for a "credibility check" on you and your business. Let's say you have a prospect who can become a customer, but who wants to talk with some of your other customers first. Standard procedure is to give the customer a list of references who will say positive things about you. I suggest you develop a list of recommenders who will promote you to the hilt and say wonderful things about you.

Recommenders should be long-term and loyal customers, but they do not always have to be. The longer they have been with you, the more they will know about your business and how you run it—that usually helps. However, a recommender can be anyone who is extremely satisfied with what you have done and is willing to be available to tell anyone else who calls.

CUSTOMER RETENTION: ONE MORE LOOK

There is no question in anyone's mind that the customer is a focal point of your business. Without customers, you have no business. So it makes sense to do everything you can to keep them loyal and committed to you for life, or at least as long as possible. This book has provided hundreds of ways to create superior customer service programs and systems for your business, to use customer service as a powerful marketing tool, and to position your business as a high quality customer service provider so customers will choose you over your competition.

This final section offers a series of reminders about the importance of proactive customer service, customer retention programs, and the effect these have on your business. It is up to you to put all these ideas into practice, to keep your customers for life. The lists at the end of this chapter are compiled from a variety of sources and modified from my experiences. Make the lists applicable for your business; make the information work for you.

Begin your journey to long-term customer retention by developing specific retention programs for your business. Make sure your efforts are proactive rather than reactive. The differences will be more clear in a moment.

Developing Customer Retention Programs

Customer service does not exist in a vacuum and neither do customer retention programs. You need an overall structure or guiding focus to make them work. Consider marketing as that guiding principle, and create all your customer retention programs under your marketing umbrella. This will enable you to track and evaluate your efforts. Once you set up the programs within your marketing plan, you can use customer service as an effective yet inexpensive marketing tool.[5]

Some companies still think of customer service as something they do after the fact. They view the process more as a complaint-handling system than as a proactive technique. As we've discussed earlier, complaint handling is only one

---

[5] *Marketing Strategies for Small Businesses,* R. F. Gerson, Crisp Publications, 1994.

small part of customer service. Decide now to develop superior customer service and retention programs that are proactive, rather than reactive.

Proactive versus Reactive Efforts

Customer service has two aspects. Reactive customer service comes after the fact—after a customer has had a problem or a complaint, is dissatisfied or has had to bring something to the attention of a business. Proactive service begins even before a customer walks in the door. Your business is already prepared to do everything possible to satisfy and keep the customer.

One of the best examples of proactive service is making the buying experience as easy as possible for the customer. Speed up the purchase process, decrease waiting times (people hate to wait), be friendly, make your business a nice place to be.

Many businesses, especially service businesses, do not have a tangible item to sell. Therefore, the office, the appearance of the facility and the people are the only tangible items the customer sees. Make them pleasant and appealing. People will continue to do business with you because they like the way you look and this makes them feel comfortable. They will also continue to buy from you because they like the way you treat them.

Proactive service and retention do wonders for a company's bottom line. "Retention-getters," such as thanking customers for coming in, thanking them for shopping even when they do not buy, and offering them additional information so that they can make a better purchase decision keeps them coming back to you, simply because you created a pleasant atmosphere, made it a nice place for them to shop and made it easy for them to buy.

Communication is another form of proactive service and customer retention. Keep in touch with your customers by phone or mail. Ask how things are going in their lives. Let them know about things you will do just for them. Make them feel special.

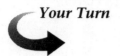

Your Turn

What are you doing now to manage your customer service and customer retention activities? Complete this chart to identify what your company is doing now. Although there are ten blank lines under each column heading in the list, you are not obligated to only completing the ten, nor are you obligated to complete the entire list if you are not doing that many things.

Proactive Management Efforts	Reactive Management Efforts
1. _____	1. _____
2. _____	2. _____
3. _____	3. _____
4. _____	4. _____
5. _____	5. _____
6. _____	6. _____
7. _____	7. _____
8. _____	8. _____
9. _____	9. _____
10. _____	10. _____

This exercise should help you to most effectively identify and develop the programs you need. Hopefully, your proactive column is longer than your reactive column. If not, you have a lot of work to do.

See how you can adapt the lists in the remainder of this chapter to make them more useful in your business.

Proactive Service Management

Here are ten things you can do to proactively manage customer service retention and customer satisfaction in your business. Doing some of them will ensure you a larger customer base; doing all of them could make you the market leader in your field. One thing is certain: when you implement these ten suggestions in your business your numbers of long-term customers and your levels of customer satisfaction will definitely increase.

1. **Everyone Works For the Customer**—Become a customer-focused organization—totally and completely. You and your employees do not work for the company; you work for the customer. Without customers, there is no business and no company. Place customers on the highest pedestal possible, and do everything you can to ensure their satisfaction.

2. **Get To Know Your Customers Intimately**—Companies that know their customers intimately are much more profitable than their competitors. This is because these companies are giving customers exactly what they want and ask for. Talk to your customers directly. Write to them. Call them. Ask them questions. Survey them. Invite them to your facility. Take them to lunch or dinner. Court them. Do anything and everything you can to learn about who they are; what they need, want and expect; and how they want you to give it to them (and put all this information into your database). Then, give it to them just that way, even if it means modifying your current product or service or policies.

3. **Build Quality In**—Once you know what your customers want from you, give it to them at the highest level of quality possible. Quality is whatever the customer says it is, and it can change daily. Build quality into your products and services from the start. Quality is like a wellness program for your business. Use good preventive techniques to ensure the "healthiest" (i.e., highest quality) product or service possible.

4. **Develop a Passionate Customer Focus**—Being customer-focused is no longer enough. That will make you barely competitive. Every company believes they are customer-focused. You must be passionate about your customers; love them as you would have them love you. Your customer-focus must be so deep and dedicated that it

permeates your personal being and the life of your business. Customers are the lifeblood of your business, so treat them with care, affection and attention.

5. **Train Your Staff**—This is one of the most critical elements in providing high-quality service and achieving customer satisfaction. Customer service and quality improvement is everyone's job, so train your staff in the technical aspects of their work as well as the service-related aspects of it. Everyone gives service to the customers, not just the "customer service department." You may want to think about not having a customer service department. This forces everyone to rely only on him or herself to take the responsibility of serving and satisfying the customer.

6. **Empower Your Staff**—Training your staff to provide superior customer service and to take the responsibility for satisfying the customers is still not enough. Empower the staff with the authority to do whatever it takes to guarantee the customer is satisfied. No passing the buck to another employee or having to get a manager's approval on a refund or an exchange. Give everyone the authority to do whatever it takes, whenever the customer wants it, to ensure total customer satisfaction. When you empower your staff, you find their commitment to their jobs, the business and the customers increases greatly.

7. **Measure, Measure, Measure**—Measure everything, for two important reasons: 1) What gets measured gets done; and 2) You must measure it to improve it. Measure the performance of yourself and your staff. Measure the quality of the products and services you produce and sell. Measure the satisfaction levels and service perceptions of your customers. Then, make the appropriate and necessary positive changes based on the results of these measurements.

8. **Recognize and Reward**—Recognize and reward both your employees and your customers. Show your employees your appreciation for a job well done. Let them know you care about them as people, not just as workers.

If you're going to treat customers as kings and queens, you must also treat your employees like royalty. Never forget that your employees are your customers too. Show your customers and your employees you appreciate them. Let them know you care about them as people also, not just as buyers and deliverers of your product or service.

When you recognize people for their efforts, the rewards should be meaningful. This does not mean they necessarily have to be monetary. People crave recognition for their efforts. I used to give out stickers that had JWD printed on them, for a "Job Well Done." I also give out smiley faces. Both things show people I care and appreciate their efforts. I send customers thank you cards, holiday cards and gifts. What do you do to recognize and reward your employees and customers?

9. **Go Out Of Your Way**—Everyone is looking for and expecting value for their money. All your competitors are trumpeting their quality service and value. Differentiate your business by going out of your way for customers. Give them as many value-added benefits as possible. Do everything you can think of to satisfy the customer, which the customer does not or would not expect from you. Take your passionate customer focus and develop it to the point that customer satisfaction is not enough. "Wow," "dazzle" and "delight" your customers. What can you do, how can you go out of your way to create what I call the "Wow Factor"? This is when customers who do business with you are so delighted that they come away saying "Wow."

10. **Make It Better**—Some businesses survey their customers and find out the customers believe they are getting quality products and services and they are very satisfied. Then, these businesses get complacent and rest on their laurels. You cannot do that in today's economy and competitive environment. If your customers tell you that your quality is excellent, your service is superb, and they are highly satisfied with the way you treat them, immediately look for ways to make everything you are doing better. If you do not, your competitors will. Then your customers will become their customers.

Service can always be improved, just as customer satisfaction levels can be increased. The increments may be ever so slight—that is why we call them continuous, incremental improvements. Do not be one of those companies that believes "if it ain't broke, don't fix it." Be one of the new breed of passionate, customer-focused companies that believes "if it ain't broke, make it better." If you do not, your competitors will, and your customers will then go to them.

Ten Commandments of Superior Customer Service

1. The customer is the most important person in the company.

2. The customer is not dependent on you—you are dependent on the customer. You work for the customer.

3. The customer is not an interruption of your work. The customer is the purpose of your work.

4. The customer does you a favor by visiting or calling your business. You are not doing the customer a favor by serving them.

5. The customer is as much a part of your business as anything else, including inventory, employees and your facility. If you sold the business, the customers would go with it.

6. The customer is not a cold statistic. The customer is a person with feelings and emotions, just like you. Treat the customer better than you want to be treated.

7. The customer is not someone to argue with or match wits with. You'll win a battle but lose the war.

8. It is your job to satisfy the needs, wants and expectations of your customers and, whenever possible, resolve their fears and complaints.

9. The customer deserves the most attentive, courteous and professional treatment you can provide.

10. The customer is the lifeblood of your business. Always remember that without customers, you would not have a business. You work for the customer.

Ten Tips for Long-Term Customer Retention

1. Call each customer by name.

2. Listen to what each customer has to say.

3. Be concerned about each customer as an individual.

4. Be courteous to each customer.

5. Be responsive to the needs of the individual customer.

6. Know your customers' personal buying histories and motivations.

7. Take sufficient time with each customer.

8. Involve customers in your business. Ask for their advice and suggestions.

9. Make customers feel important. Pay them compliments.

10. Listen first to understand the customer. Then, speak so they can understand you.

Customer's Bill of Rights

The customer has a right to:

▶ Professional, courteous and prompt service

▶ Your full and undivided attention each time the customer chooses to do business with you

▶ Quality products and services

▶ Fulfillment of needs in a manner consistent with reasonable service expectations

▶ Competent, knowledgeable and well-trained staff

- ▶ Attention to every detail every time they access your customer service system

- ▶ The benefits of all your resources, teamwork and networks to provide superior, long-term service

- ▶ Open channels of communication for feedback, complaints and compliments

- ▶ A fair price for your products and services

- ▶ Appreciation from you and your staff for past and future business

Seven Points to Successful Customer Retention

✔ 1. Have a clear customer service mission, vision and philosophy. Communicate this to your employees, then train and empower them to carry out your service mission.

✔ 2. Provide customers with quality products, services and care.

✔ 3. Listen closely to your customers, and then act on their suggestions. Do the same for your employees.

✔ 4. Pay attention to your own intuition when serving customers, and have your employees pay attention to their own intuitions.

✔ 5. Treat customers with respect, trust, fairness, honesty and integrity.

✔ 6. Communicate with your customers regularly, including current customers, former customers and your competitor's customers.

✔ 7. Expand your product and service offerings carefully, ensuring that you can continue to provide quality customer service while you grow.

ASK YOURSELF

► What is the lifetime value of your customers?

► Identify five things you are doing to maintain customer loyalty.

► Describe the types of customer retention programs you use.

FINAL THOUGHTS

Customer service can always be improved, which will lead to ever-increasing levels of customer satisfaction. Never think, for one moment, that you can sit back just because your latest survey told you your customers were satisfied. If you know they are satisfied, you have to find out how to make them more satisfied.

We know for a fact that customers will appreciate your efforts and your thank yous (cards, gifts, other rewards). There is something else you must do to make sure customers stay with you and remain loyal: Increase the perceived value of their psychological switching costs.

What this means is that it usually does not take a great deal of money for a customer to begin buying the same product or service from another supplier. But, if the customer is psychologically "attached" to a provider (hopefully your business) for any number of reasons, the psychological costs associated with switching to your competitor becomes too great. Here are some of the themes I've heard in interviews with my clients' customers on this topic:

"They treat me like family."

"They know my name."

"They sent me a birthday card."

"They really do appreciate my business."

"They always pay attention to me when I come in to shop. The staff never gets impatient, even when I don't know exactly what I want."

You get the idea. There is a strong psychological component to customer service and long-term customer retention. Each of the above comments relates to fulfilling a psychological need, such as feeling important or appreciated, of being recognized, and of being included. If you looked at your own business and customers, you can probably identify other psychological needs that you can fill.

Customers are the lifeblood of your business. Service is the vehicle that keeps the blood pumping. Superior customer service, proactive retention programs, using service as a marketing tool, and going out of your way to get, satisfy and keep your customers will make your business successful.

ABOUT THE AUTHOR

Dr. Richard F. Gerson is President of Gerson Goodson, Inc., a marketing and management consulting firm that also provides corporate training programs to its clients. He received his Ph.D. from Florida State University in 1978, and has been consulting with individual entrepreneurs, small businesses, and several Fortune 500 firms ever since. Dr. Gerson is a Certified Management Consultant, a Certified Professional Consultant and a Certified Professional Sales Person.

Dr. Gerson is a nationally renowned author, speaker and trainer. He has written 12 books that have been translated into 8 foreign languages, and he has published over 300 popular and professional articles for journals, magazines, newspapers and newsletters.

If you have any questions about this book or any of Dr. Gerson's other works, or about his availability as a speaker/consultant/trainer, call him at (813) 726-7619 or write to him at 2451 McMullen Booth Road, Ste. 205, Clearwater, Florida 34619.

THE U.S. CHAMBER OF COMMERCE
SMALL BUSINESS INSTITUTE

We hope that you found this book beneficial to the success of your operation. For additional materials from the Small Business Institute, refer to the listing below. A free catalog is available upon request from the Small Business Institute, 1200 Hamilton Court, Menlo Park, California 94025. Phone: 800-884-2880

While you are learning, you can also earn a Small Business Institute Certificate of Completion along with valuable continuing education units (CEUs).

Course materials:	Order Numbers:
Marketing and Sales	
Marketing Strategies for Small Businesses	172-4
Prospecting: The Key to Sales Success	271-2
Direct Mail Magic	075-2
Professional Selling	42-4
Writing and Implementing a Marketing Plan	083-3
Budget and Finance	
Financial Basics of Small Business Success	167-8
Budgeting for a Small Business	171-6
Extending Credit and Collecting Cash	168-6
Getting a Business Loan	164-3
Personal Financial Fitness	205-4
Legal Issues	
A Legal Guide for Small Business	266-6
A Manager's Guide to OSHA	180-5
Rightful Termination: Avoiding Litigation	248-8
Sexual Harassment: What You Need to Know	312-3
The A.D.A.: Hiring, Accommodating and Supervising Employees with Disabilities	311-5
Human Relations and Communications	
Human Relations in Small Business	185-6
Attacking Absenteeism	42-6
Quality Interviewing	262-3

The publisher of books for the U.S. Chamber of Commerce Small Business Institute is Crisp Publications. Crisp offers over 200 other business and entrepreneurship titles. For more information, call the U.S. Chamber of Commerce Small Business Institute at 800-884-2880.